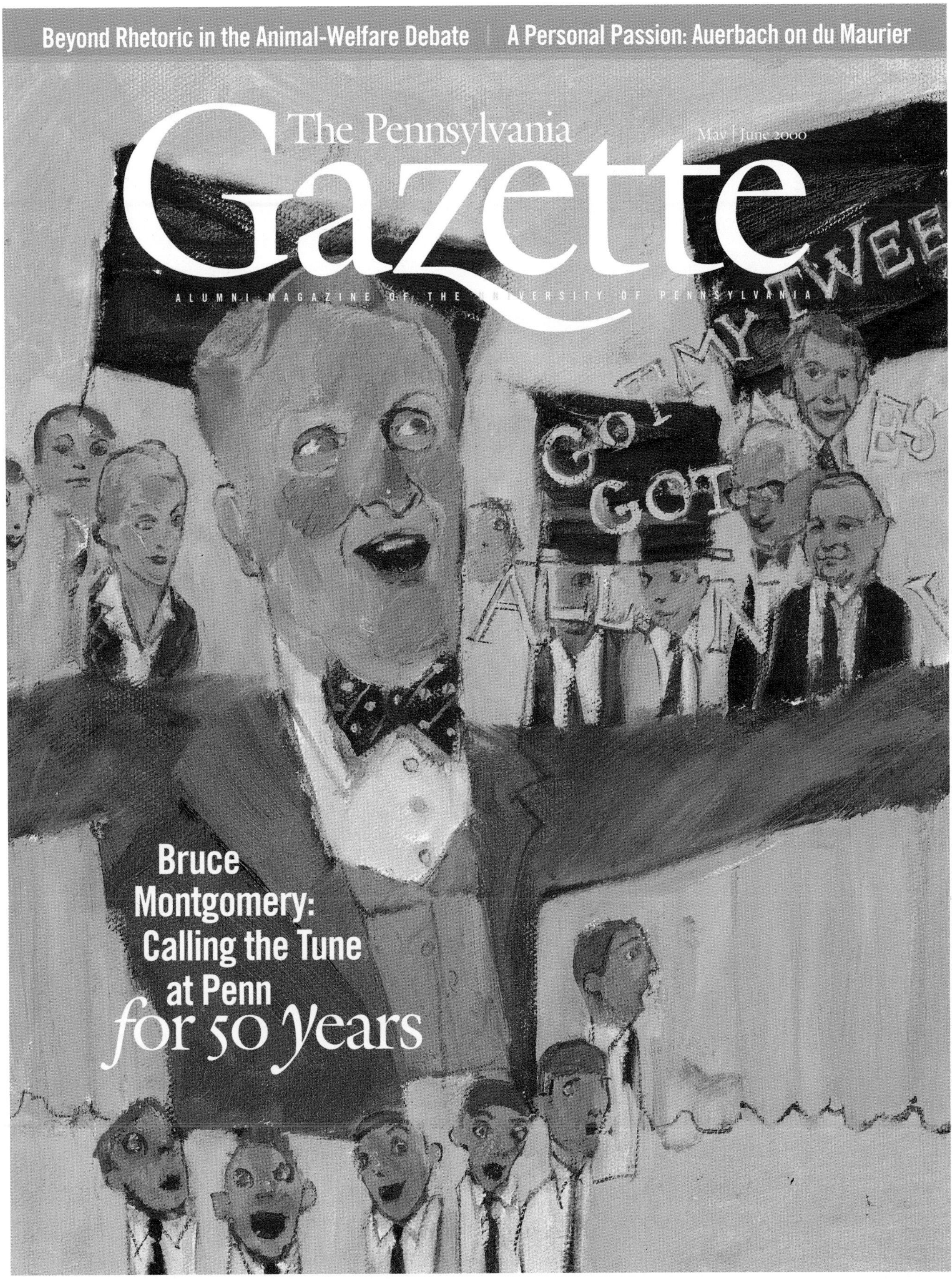

Beyond Rhetoric in the Animal-Welfare Debate | A Personal Passion: Auerbach on du Maurier

The Pennsylvania
Gazette

May | June 2000

ALUMNI MAGAZINE OF THE UNIVERSITY OF PENNSYLVANIA

Bruce
Montgomery:
Calling the Tune
at Penn
for 50 years

Cover: *The Pennsylvania Gazette* – May/June 2000
Used with permission of *The Pennsylvania Gazette*

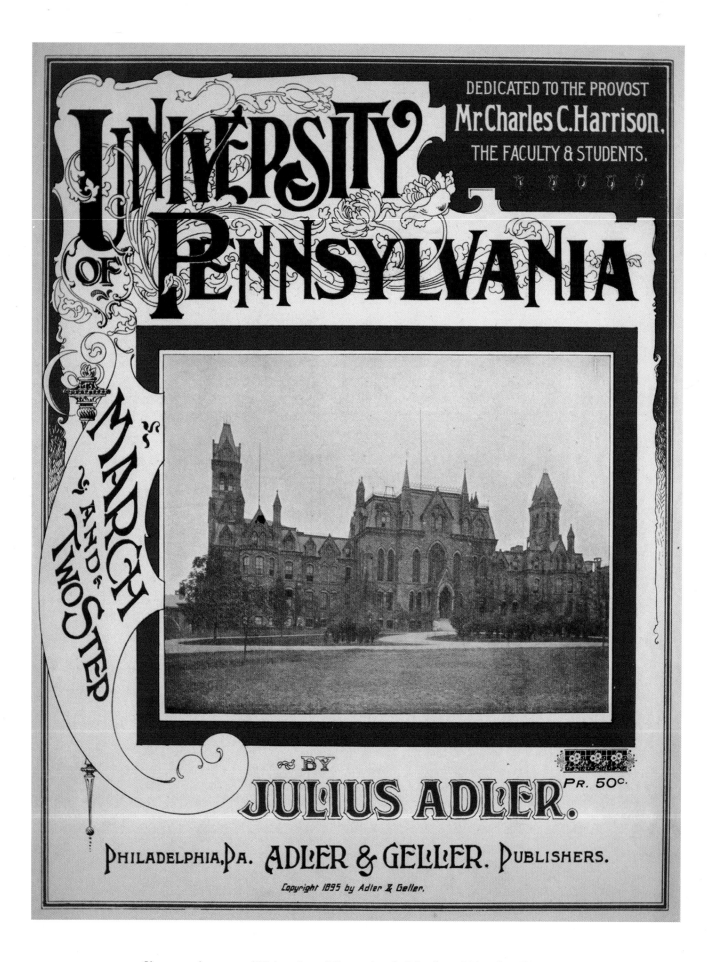

Sheet music cover: "University of Pennsylvania March and Two Step" – 1899
Used with permission of University Archives and Records Center, University of Pennsylvania

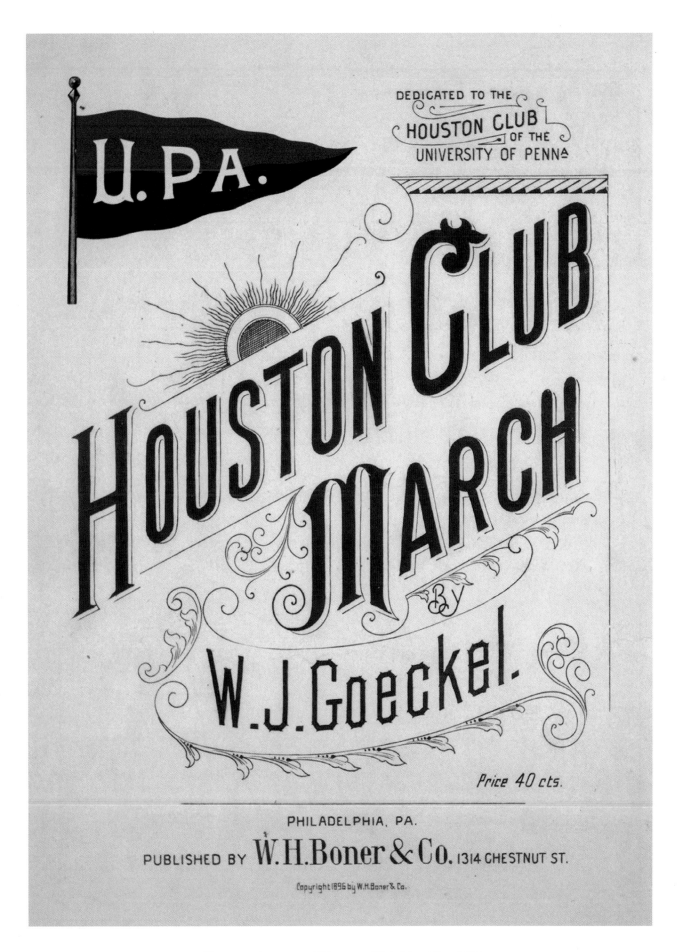

Sheet music cover: "Houston Club March" – 1896
Used with permission of University Archives and Records Center, University of Pennsylvania

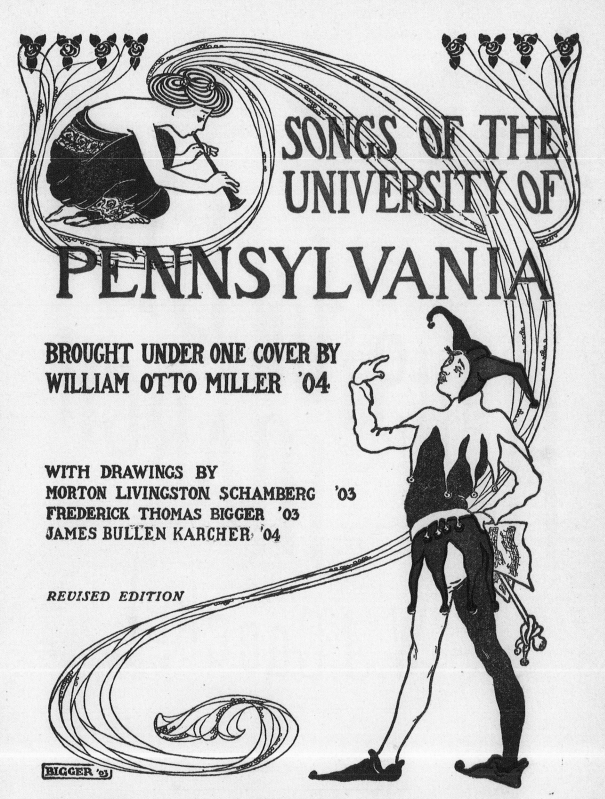

Title page: *Songs of the University of Pennsylvania* – 1903 Edition
Used with permission of University Archives and Record Center, University of Pennsylvania

Program cover: Mask and Wig 8th annual production, *No Gentleman of France* – 1896
Designed by Maxfield Parrish – Used with permission of Mask and Wig

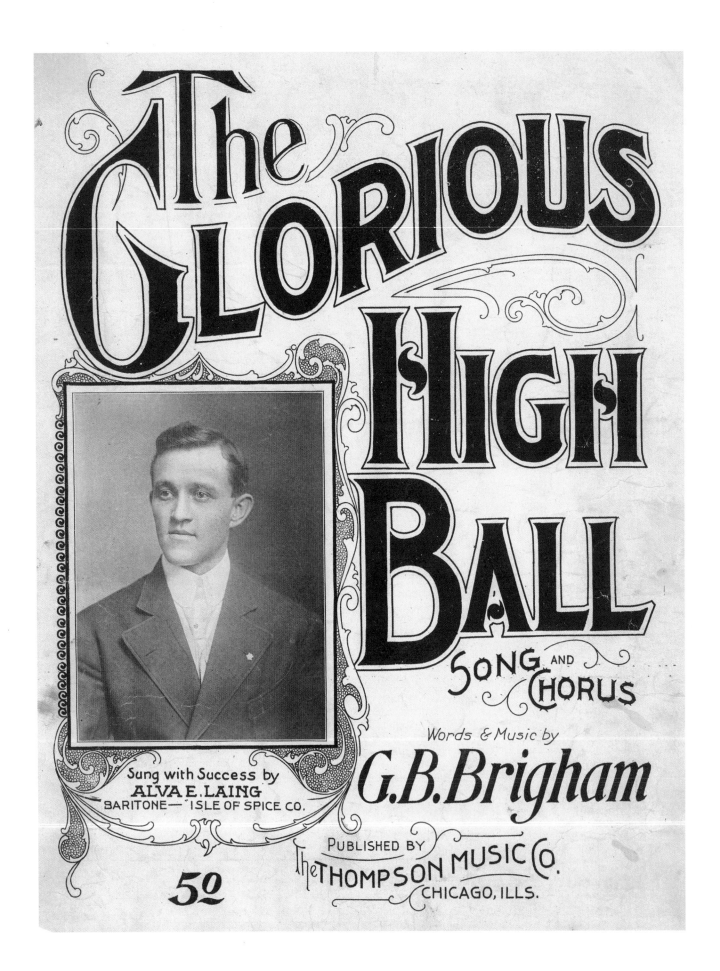

Sheet music cover: "The Glorious High Ball" – 1903
Used with Permission of Bruce Montgomery Foundation for the Arts

Program cover: Mask and Wig 9th annual production, *Very Little Red Riding Hood* – 1897
Designed by Maxfield Parrish – Used with permission of Mask and Wig

Sheet music cover: "Old Pennsylvania" – 1923
Autographed by Clay Boland and Frank Winegar, Composer/Lyricists
Used with permission of Michel Huber

SONGS of PENN
Honoring Musical Tradition at the University of Pennsylvania

A COLLECTION OF SONGS WITH HISTORICAL ANNOTATIONS
COMPILED, WRITTEN *&* EDITED
BY BRUCE MONTGOMERY, 2006

Published by the Bruce Montgomery Foundation for the Arts
P.O. Box 1565
Blue Bell, PA 19422

Library of Congress Control Number: 2013936087
ISBN Number: 978-0-989 1226-0-3

Illustrations by Bruce Montgomery
Dust jacket designed by Nicholas B. Thomas, Jr.
Book Design by Jenny Young, ADVERTISING Without the Agency

Benjamin Franklin Image on cover used with permission of
University Archives & Records Center
University of Pennsylvania

Printed in the United States of America by Maple Press – York, Pennsylvania

All sales of Songs of Penn *support the*
Fellowships & Grants Program of the
Bruce Montgomery Foundation for the Arts

TO THE

University of Pennsylvania

Foreword

Rare is the person who truly lives with passion.

Rarer still is one who devotes 50 years to that passion.

Rarest of all is he who – if given the choice – would do it all over again.

Bruce "Monty" Montgomery was that person, and *Songs of Penn* captures his spirit

and the very heart of what brought him joy: music.

This wonderful book celebrates that which lives on for eternity, the musical compositions,

the harmonies, and the ties that build incredible connections like those Monty had

with the University of Pennsylvania.

The entire campus community welcomes *Songs of Penn*,

and the gems within it will continue to remind us of our pride for the Red and Blue.

As a legacy and treasure trove for us to share with each other,

our families, and the world, this book will keep the musical traditions of Penn

alive on campus and in our homes for years to come.

Amy Gutmann
President and Christopher H. Browne
Distinguished Professor of Political Science

SONGS *of* PENN

Honoring Musical Tradition at the University of Pennsylvania

A COLLECTION OF SONGS WITH HISTORICAL ANNOTATIONS

COMPILED, WRITTEN & EDITED

BY

BRUCE MONTGOMERY

Table of Contents

Songs & Historical Annotations

Alphabetical Index of First Lines

In some cases, the Index of First Lines contains two or more entries for a given song. The actual first line generally is to the verse of the song and is not always as familiar as the chorus, which often is the only portion still sung today. In these instances, therefore, I have made separate entries for each.

A message from the
Bruce Montgomery Foundation for the Arts

Bruce Montgomery – often described in the press as "Philadelphia's Renaissance Man" – was an iconic figure at the University of Pennsylvania, directing and mentoring thousands of students for half a century from 1950 to 2000. Born in 1927, he spent forty-four of his years at Penn as Director of the Penn Glee Club, enhancing the University's prestige at home and abroad through numerous concert tours around the world. During his tenure at Penn "Monty" also directed Mask & Wig, Penn Players, Penn Singers, the Penn Band, and inspired the formation of many additional performing arts groups on campus.

Upon his retirement in 2000, Monty finally had time to devote to a decades-old project that several trustees and faculty members had urged him to complete. More than eighty years after the last publication of a Penn songbook, they believed it was time for a new edition. This would enable the University to accomplish its goal of keeping alive the musical traditions that had been an integral part of its heritage for more than two-and-a-half centuries. As the new millennium began, Monty stepped up his earlier sporadic efforts to collect, research, edit and historically annotate the manuscript for *Songs of Penn.* He completed the book shortly before his passing in 2008, at the age of eighty-one.

The wealth of material that Monty left behind, including the manuscript for this book, was one of the important factors in the decision by his family, in 2010, to establish the Bruce Montgomery Foundation for the Arts as a tax-exempt, not-for-profit 501(c)(3) public charity. Its mission is to continue his legacy by awarding annual grants to talented students and organizations pursuing excellence in the performing arts. To help support this mission, Monty's estate transferred ownership of all his prolific intellectual property to the Foundation. Now all royalties, licensing fees and sales revenues from his published and yet-to-be published work help fund the organization's endowment for its Fellowships & Grants Program.

Songs of Penn is the Foundation's first major project. This volume serves as a toast to Penn – one of the nation's first and most prestigious universities – and to its musical traditions; it is also a tribute to Bruce Montgomery's memory. What follows is Monty's original work. Any notes written in the present tense remain as he wrote them and represent his life-long devotion to the University of Pennsylvania and to the students he loved so much.

Bruce Eglinton Montgomery
June 20, 1927 - June 20, 2008

Preface

Songs of the University of Pennsylvania have appeared in book form since the Penn Glee Club first published a small volume of thirty-four songs in 1879. It was edited by Hugh A. Clarke, a member of the music faculty and the Club's long-time director (or "Leader" as he was then called). Nine of the songs were simply lyrics written to existing tunes. They were published without the music, which presumably was known to all. Eight were class songs (including the provocative "Cremation Song of 1881," sung to the air: "Flee as a Bird"). Some were in Latin either in whole, such as "Lauriger Horatius," or in part. Others, such as "The Last Cigar" and "Oh, the Bull-dog On the Bank," were simply popular songs of the day and had nothing to do with Penn or academia *per se.*

Collections of songs of the University were published again in 1903, 1909, 1916 and 1923. But this sixth volume is the first to contain notes on the historical background of each song; it also includes my personal experience with this rich material. Some information you may already know; some will be of passing interest; some may delight and surprise you! There are a number of songs here that were written after 1923. There are also a few included simply because some record of them ought to be acknowledged. Should an even deeper retrospective be undertaken in the future, the writer may depend on this book as a resource. There are songs here that are sung regularly, but have never made it into print before. Can you believe that one of Penn's most popular songs, "Drink a Highball," never appeared until now? Well, it is finally here and its history will astonish you because it refutes so much of our traditional "knowledge" about the song.

Here, then, are fifty-five *Songs of Penn.* The research has been great fun. Enjoy these songs for themselves – but also enjoy them by learning a little more about their history.

Introduction

The last official songbook of the University of Pennsylvania, published way back in 1923, has been out-of-print for many years. A long-time pet project of mine has been to gather and arrange a new volume of the *Songs of Penn*. As Director of the Penn Glee Club, I considered this appropriate since the very first collection of Penn songs was published by the Glee Club in 1879. Furthermore, the entire history of these songs has been closely connected to their introduction and perpetuation by the Glee Club, the Penn Band, or both.

Music – both academic and extracurricular – occupies an important and vigorous place at the University today. This builds on a tradition that harks back to the very beginnings of the institution. Consider the following: Francis Hopkinson, a member of the Class of 1757, and a signer of the Declaration of Indepenedence, is generally acknowledged as America's first native-born composer of consequence. While his "With Jemmie On the Sea" is not specifically a University song, it is included in this volume because of its historical significance and its early popularity at Penn. His son, Joseph Hopkinson (Class of 1786), was also a prominent composer.

In September, 1784 Yale's president, Ezra Stiles, journeyed to Philadelphia to receive an honorary degree from the University of Pennsylvania. He was so impressed with the fact that the Penn students managed to present two very elaborate programs of instrumental music, he wrote about them in detail in his journal, referring to the use of "bassons, clarionets, etc."

Thomas Dunn English (College 1839) wrote "Ben Bolt" and it became one of the most popular American songs of the 19th century. It, too, is included in this volume for historical reasons since it was frequently sung on campus in its early days. Hugh A. Clarke, the aforementioned director of the Glee Club, wrote music for the Greek dramas produced by University students in 1885 and 1903. And dozens of original songs widely popular in the 1930's and '40's were written for Mask & Wig productions spanning more than a century, including several by Moses "Moe" Jaffe (1923), Clay Boland (1926), and Robert W. Troup, Jr. (1941).

For the *Mask of American Drama*, presented by the Philomathean and Zelosophic Societies of the University in 1917, there was an entire volume of original lyrics for which the popular operetta composer Reginald de Koven wrote the music. The lyrics of the light opera, *Hades, Inc.*, were written by William O. Miller (1904), with music by H. Alexander Matthews, then director of the Glee Club. In addition to writing a new show each year for the Penn Glee Club, I was the composer/lyricist/librettist for *Spindrift* and *Why Me?* – two of many musicals presented by the Penn Players (Penn's major theatrical group) or the Penn Singers (Penn's light opera company) and directed by me for over half a century. I was also the composer/lyricist for the 1964 Off-Broadway hit, *The Amorous Flea*. Although this show was not written specifically for Penn students (unlike the first two just mentioned), the Penn Players staged *"Flea's"* first amateur production on campus in 1966 after its professional New York and Los Angeles runs.

On several occasions the famous "March King," John Phillip Sousa, conducted the Penn Band. His last concert at the University was on November 21, 1930. Of this event the eminent Penn musicologist and historian George E. Nitzsche related: "After conducting the Penn Band in a number of his own marches, we asked him to conduct the 'University of Pennsylvania Band March,' which Roland F. Seitz, of Glen Rock, Pa., composed for the University Band in 1901. Mr. Sousa turned to me and asked 'Do I know it?' I answered, 'Of course you do' and so he conducted. Afterwards, with a twinkle in his eyes, he said 'That is one of the best marches, aside from my own productions, I have ever conducted.'" The fine words "Hail, Alma Mater, thy sons cheer thee now…" were added for the trio of the march by Magruder Craighead (College 1903).

Another great work, the "Franklin Field March," was composed by the famous band director Edwin Franco Goldman. George E. Nitzsche wrote the words for the trio and, once again, we are indebted to him for his recollection of its debut performance. "Goldman's 'Franklin Field March'," he related in Franklin Field Illustrated (October 18, 1940, Vol. 25, No. 3), "was played for the first time in public at Franklin Field on November 5, 1932, on the occasion of the annual Penn vs. Pittsburgh football game. The combined bands of the two universities, numbering nearly 400 men and spreading over three-fourths of the field, performed under the personal direction of the composer, who at the same time formally dedicated this great March to the University. This was one of the most thrilling and spectacular episodes ever staged on a football field, and the March proved an instant success." Remember, this was before television and the giant Super Bowl extravaganzas!

When Ben McGivern (Wharton 1923), and David Zoob (College 1923) wrote the words and music, respectively, for "Fight On, Pennsylvania!" little did they know that they had created one of the all-time great American college songs. Their march ranks today as one of the three or four most popular songs of Penn and has long since transcended its authors' original intention as a football song. It is now played at virtually every sporting event at Penn.

On a personal note, there was a certain ironic twist to the fact that I – who have concerned myself with vocal music for my entire professional life – composed the "University of Pennsylvania Glee Club March (PENNy-Whistle)" for the Club's 125th anniversary without a vocal part. In place of a vocal trio, which would have been logical for a work honoring a chorus, I had the entire Glee Club *whistling* a counterpoint theme! The work made its debut on Franklin Field on October 25, 1986. It was performed by the combined Penn Band and Glee Club – with nary a vocalized word – at the Yale-Penn Homecoming football game. I greatly enjoyed the honor and thrill of conducting it that day on the field.

During the last half of the 19th century, and well into the 20th, most University singing depended upon the Penn Glee Club as a nucleus. As a result, the songs of that period were usually written for male voices in four parts. Penn's long-held allegiance to such traditional collegiate songs as "Gaudeamus Igitur" and "Integer Vitae" gave way to original songs composed especially for Penn. Outstanding lyrics for Penn songs have been written over the years by such representative students and faculty as: S. Weir Mitchell, William O. Miller, Isaac Hampshur Jones, Edward Mumford, Arthur Hobson Quinn, Vincent Brecht and Arthur L. Church. The music has been of an equally high standard, written by such fine Pennsylvania composers as William J. Goeckel, Edward McCollin, Hugh Clarke, H. Alexander Matthews, David Zoob and Morrison Boyd.

Robert A. Doane (1942) and Edward L. Foley (1935) wrote the "University of Pennsylvania Bicentennial March," winning a competition for that 1940 milestone's official song. Later, in 1990, I was commissioned by the University to compose the "Academic Festive Anthem" for band and chorus, based on a text by Benjamin Franklin. The work was performed at Commencement on Franklin Field to celebrate Penn's 250th anniversary in 1990. At the time I couldn't have foreseen that it would become a frequently performed anthem for future Commencements and other festive occasions.

Today, as throughout the University's history, music plays a vital role in Penn's enduring traditions and continuing growth. The Band and the Glee Club remain the primary performers of specifically Penn music but to these have been added, as of this writing [2006], an even dozen all-male, all-female and co-ed *a cappella* singing groups; a half dozen musical theatre groups; two dance ensembles; four regular instrumental groups, innumerable rock-and-roll bands; and countless "pick-up" ensembles who need nothing more than a dormitory room and perhaps a guitar. The Penn Glee Club has transported songs of the University of Pennsylvania throughout the world to presidents, emperors, kings and commoners. And the Penn Band has graced football stadiums and arenas around the country with Penn's great marches and fight songs.

For more than two-and-a-half centuries, members of the Penn community have made music together. In a foreword to the 1923 edition of *Songs of the University of Pennsylvania*, then provost Josiah H. Penniman wrote that "the sentiment of days gone by lingers in the songs that were sung and nothing is more powerful in recreating the past." It is my fervent hope that this new volume of *Songs of Penn* will evoke powerful memories and lead future generations of students, faculty, administrators and alumni to a renewed appreciation of Penn's rich musical heritage.

Bruce Montgomery
Director
University of Pennsylvania Glee Club
1956-2000

A Note About The Songs

Nearly all of the songs that follow are arranged for solo melody and piano accompaniment.
The rare exceptions are compositions usually sung *a cappella*. Even these, however, have been given
a solo rendering with piano accompaniment.

When choral arrangements appear, they are written for either
mixed or male chorus. In arrangements for male voices, the tenor parts in the treble clef
are sung or played one full octave lower than written.

Leading off with "Hail Pennsylvania" (Penn's Alma Mater)
and ending with "Afterglow," the songs follow a loose order based on frequency of performance,
popularity, or appropriateness to specific occasions.

Since most of the songs were taken from one or more of the five previous editions of
Penn songbooks dating back to 1879, notational variances abound.
Modern technology has been applied to the music and text of this book
to assure visual consistency. However, an editorial decision was made to retain
certain idiosyncrasies found in earlier editions with regard to dynamic markings
and tempo indications (or the absence thereof), text punctuation and capitalization, etc.,
thus preserving their inherent charm.

For a complete listing of songs that appeared in previous editions, but were not selected
for *Songs of Penn*, please refer to page 181.

HAIL, PENNSYLVANIA ♫

This stirring and familiar hymn tune, originally Czarist Russia's National Anthem, is the official alma mater of the University of Pennsylvania. The words were written by Edgar M. Dilley when he was assistant student director of the Penn Glee Club. The song was awarded a prize of $25.00 by an Alumni Committee of which Edward G. McCollin, College 1878, himself a respected composer, was chairman. Its first public performance was by the Glee Club in 1895 at the Academy of Music – Philadelphia's famous opera house – conducted by young Mr. Dilley. Among my earliest recollections as a young boy was watching the visor-capped, long-coated Penn Band lining up at the goal line of Franklin Field at football games, trumpets playing the lively fanfare from Tchaikovsky's "1812 Overture," and then the whole formation stepping off to this marvelous hymn in quick-march time. This apparently pleased Edgar Dilley for he claimed that both "The Red and Blue" and his "Hail, Pennsylvania" were written "to be sung rapidly and with spirit." He bemoaned the fact that both songs were generally performed too slowly.

HAIL, PENNSYLVANIA
THE UNIVERSITY OF PENNSYLVANIA ALMA MATER

Words by
EDGAR M. DILLEY 1897

Music by
ALEXIS LVOV

HAIL, PENNSYLVANIA
THE UNIVERSITY OF PENNSYLVANIA ALMA MATER

Words by
EDGAR M. DILLEY 1897

Music by
ALEXIS LVOV
Arr. by
BRUCE MONTGOMERY

Hail! Penn - syl - va - ni - a! No - ble and strong; To thee with loy - al hearts, We raise our song. Swell - ing to Heav - ven Loud our prais - es ring; Hail! Penn - syl - va - ni - a, Of thee we sing!

HAIL, PENNSYLVANIA

THE UNIVERSITY OF PENNSYLVANIA ALMA MATER

Words by
EDGAR M. DILLEY 1897

Music by
ALEXIS LVOV
Arr. by
BRUCE MONTGOMERY

Maestoso

Hail! Penn - syl - va - ni - a! No - ble and strong; To

thee with loy - al hearts, We raise our song.

*

Swell - ing to Heav - en____ Loud our prais - es ring;____

Hail! Penn - syl - va - ni - a, Of thee we sing!

*The prosody of this measure and the next differs from the
original so that a more musical effect is given to the lyric.
This is the version sung and recorded by the Glee Club.*

Grandstand denizens singing "The Red and Blue": Penn vs. Gettysburg – 1912
Used with permission – University Archives & Records Center – University of Pennsylvania

CHEER, PENNSYLVANIA

This Penn song is unique among all of the University's songs in that the march, once popular in its entirety, is now known only for its "trio" – the melodic final section. This is the only part played today by the Penn Band; the only section sung by the Glee Club; and the only section played on the chimes after a football win. Former band director Claude White made an arrangement of the entire march for the University's 250th Anniversary in 1990. While historically intriguing, the full march "did not meet with overwhelming enthusiasm!" he stated to me. "The trio is much the best part of the march and deserves to stand on its own." Written in 1906, I imagine the composer would be happy to know that at least a part of his creation has survived.

CHEER, PENNSYLVANIA

Words & Music by
C.W. O'CONNOR

Intro.

Moderato

Trio

Cheer, Penn - syl - va - nia, Cheer ev - er -

-more,_____ We're here to see the

Red and Blue score and score;_____ and when we
give a re- sound- ing Hoo-
-rah, Hoo- rah,_____ Ev- er loy- al
to old Penn- syl- van- i- a._____

f

cresc.

cresc.

Fine

THE FIELD CRY OF PENN (Hang Jeff Davis)

Set to an 1858 Methodist hymn tune, this nonsense lyric first appears in the 1903 edition of the Penn songbook but its association with the University goes back farther than that. The original hymn, "Say, Brothers Will You Meet Us" – with music attributed to William Steffe – was set with the familiar "John Brown's Body" words by C. S. Hall in about 1860 and quickly became popular among Northern soldiers in the early days of the Civil War, even though the John Brown of the song was not the John Brown of Harper's Ferry fame. There is a legend (most likely apocryphal) that Julia Ward Howe first heard the tune being sung by Penn students outside the Union League in Philadelphia and wrote her famous "The Battle Hymn of the Republic" lyric based upon that occasion. For the record, she actually heard it first while visiting Union camps in 1861 in Washington, DC, and wrote her lyric there at Willard's Hotel. Exactly when the "Hang Jeff Davis" words were adapted to the song no one knows, but based on the first line, it too was during the Civil War. Dr. George E. Nitzsche wrote an impassioned plea many years ago for someone to re-write the first line "for this spirited song – one that will not be offensive to anyone or to any section of our country." Today, far more serious objections are raised by a vulgar interpolation by students using the "F" word, which has temporarily suspended its use on campus. Traditionally, the song has been played and sung immediately after Penn's football team scores a touchdown or a field goal. Its singing has always been followed by a boisterous ticking off of the number of points accrued by the team.

* Note: *Since the writing of this book, Dr. C. Erik Nordgren, Director of the Penn Glee Club since the year 2000, has discovered that the song's nonsensical lyrics actually had their origins in various popular song titles of the day, strung together in no particular order to fit with the tune of "John Brown's Body."*

THE FIELD CRY OF PENN

Authorship Unknown

Music by
WILLIAM STEFFE

THE PENNSYLVANIA GIRL

COPYRIGHT, 1903, BY HINDS & NOBLE

SEE PAGE ?

"The Pennsylvania Girl" from *Songs of the University of Pennsylvania* – 1903 Edition
Used with permission – University Archives & Records Center – University of Pennsylvania

THE PENNSYLVANIA GIRL

Words by
EDWARD W. MUMFORD 1889

Music by
EDWARD G. McCOLLIN 1878

1. If you've es-sayed to find the maid, More dear than all the rest,___ You'll know her by the hom-age paid, By all who know her best. You'll tell her by her bon-ny eye, Her heart, so warm and true,___ But

2. One col-or dyes her laugh-ing eyes, Her lips the oth-er know,___ And just a-bove her heart there lies The dain-ty silk-en bow, To show while there they rest en-shrined, There's one who holds them fast,___ Thro'

3. And so while dear old Penn shall stand A-mong her loy-al host,___ From heart to heart through-out the land, Shall ring this tri-ple toast. We'll hail the col-lege un-dis-mayed, The fair-est flag, un-furl,___ And

first of all you'll know her by The loy - al Red and Blue. Of
good, thro' ill, till lau - rel twined The col - ors wave at last. Of
with them pledge the sweet - est maid, The Penn - syl - va - nia girl. Tho'

Tempo di Valse

all that's best from East to West She is the queen, the pearl,_____
all that's rare, of all that's fair, She is the queen, the pearl,_____
some be fair, yet none com - pare To thee, the queen, the pearl,_____

Tempo di Valse

___ The maid to whom our hearts are true, The Penn - syl - va - nia
___ The maid to whom our hearts are true, The Penn - syl - va - nia
___ For ev - er true our hearts shall be, Dear Penn - syl - va - nia

girl,_____ Of all that's best, from East to West She is the
girl,_____ Of all that's rare, of all that's fair, She is the
girl,_____ For ev - er true our hearts shall be, To thee, the

THE PENNSYLVANIA GIRL

Edward W. Mumford, College 1889, and Edward G. McCollin, College 1878, wrote this song for the Penn Glee Club in July, 1893. The song book of 1903 displayed an idealized drawing of The Pennsylvania Girl as its frontispiece. Displaying an upswept hairdo and bare shoulders – more than a little reminiscent of the charming and familiar works of Charles Dana Gibson (famous for his "Gibson Girls") – the drawing was done by Morton Livingston Schamberg, Class of 1903.

EVENING SONG IN THE TRIANGLE

Words by
WILLIAM OTTO MILLER 1904

Music by
PRESTON WARE OREM 1887

1. Slow - ly the sun to the west - ward is fad - ing, The shad - ows are creep - ing a - long the south wall; The moon o'er the Old Field its soft light is shed - ding, While the bird in the eaves hears its mate's ves - per call. Like stars the lights one by one now are beam - ing, And soft tink - ling mu - sic sal - utes the bowed ear; In dark - ness I lie on the

grass fond-ly dream-ing Of all the bright days_ of the past col-lege year._

Tempo di valse

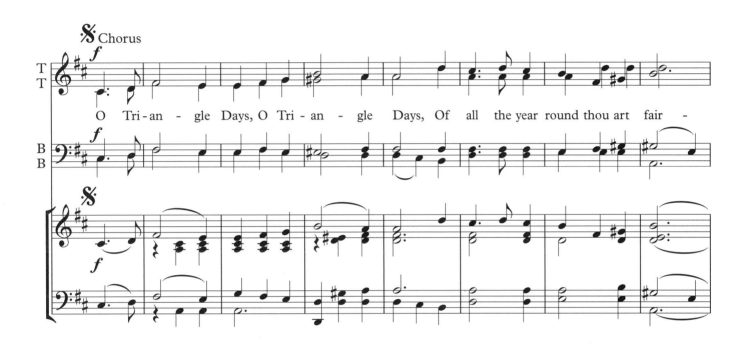

Chorus

O Tri - an - gle Days, O Tri - an - gle Days, Of all the year round thou art fair -

-est, O Tri - an - gle Days, O Tri - an - gle Days, Our song to thee we raise._

Fine

25

Moderato

Solo

2. Clear o'er the arch - es I hear a voice ring - ing With "Hail Penn - syl - va - ni - a," "Hur - rah! for the Red and the Blue;" While in - to the cho - rus a hun - dred throats swing - ing Peal out in their pride for those col - ors so true. Though years roll be - tween us no dis - tance can ev - er Dis - pel the true love which her fel - low - ship brings. We'll pledge her our loy - al - ty

now and for-ev - er While round her like i - vy fond mem-o-ry clings.

EVENING SONG IN THE TRIANGLE

William Otto Miller, Class of 1904, gathered the songs of Penn together in the popular songbook of 1903 – the first such volume since the original songbook published by the Glee Club in 1879 and edited by its director, Hugh Clarke. The words of this sweetly sentimental song hark back to a simpler and more tranquil era. It was a time when a pleasant spring evening was often spent sitting in the triangle at the west end of the college dormitory. Here spontaneous singing was the norm and, at the prodding and leadership of members of the Glee Club who lived there, full choral numbers often were heard echoing among the ivied brick walls

Cover of sheet music for University of Pennsylvania Band March – 1930
Used with permission – Penn Band Archives

THE UNIVERSITY OF PENNSYLVANIA BAND MARCH

This superb march was composed in 1901 by Roland F. Seitz, of Glen Rock, Pennsylvania. It is widely known as one of the finest marches of any college or university in the country. I mentioned it in the introduction to this volume, but it is worth quoting again, that when the great John Phillip Sousa conducted the Penn Band in a performance of it, he remarked "That is one of the best band marches, aside from my own productions, I have ever conducted." Magruder Craighead, College 1903, added the words for the trio of the piece.

THE UNIVERSITY OF PENNSYLVANIA BAND MARCH

Words by
MAGRUDER CRAIGHEAD 1906

Music by
ROLAND F. SEITZ

29

John Philip Sousa at Penn to conduct Seitz's "University of Pennsylvania Band March" –
Student Triangle – November 21, 1930
Used with permission – University Archives & Records Center – University of Pennsylvania

FIGHT ON, PENNSYLVANIA

Ben McGivern, Wharton 1923, and David Zoob, College 1923, wrote this enduring song when they were freshmen at Pennsylvania. At the time Zoob was accompanist for the Glee Club. In fairly regular correspondence with the composer in preparation for this book, I was delighted to learn that he and McGivern never ceased to be astonished that their early effort had become the "standard" that it remains today. Actually intended to be solely a football song, it is now sung at every game of every sport and has been performed around the world by the Penn Glee Club. Not long before he died in 1989, David Zoob wrote to me about "a minor incident" to include in this new songbook. "Shortly after I composed 'Fight On, Pennsylvania' (1919-1920) I was asked by the then musical director of the Glee Club to add music for a verse and did so. As I understood him, he wanted a complete number for Glee Club performances, and thus we have the song as it exists today." The composer's additional work notwithstanding, the Glee Club today performs the song almost whenever it sings – but never with the verse that he so thoughtfully added!

FIGHT ON, PENNSYLVANIA

Words by
BEN S. McGIVERAN 1923

Music by
DAVID ZOOB 1923

Fight! you Penn - syl - va - nians, There it goes a - cross this time. Red and Blue, we're with you, And we're cheer - ing for your men;_____ Then_ Fight! Fight! Fight! Penn-syl - va - ni - a, Fight on_____ for PENN! PENN!_____

rit.

a tempo

34

A TOAST TO OLD PENN

Words and Music by
ISAAC HAMPSHUR JONES 1906

A TOAST TO OLD PENN

This song was lovingly dedicated to the Glee Club when its composer-lyricist was a junior at Penn in 1905 and serving as the undergraduate leader of the Club. While it no longer is performed, the song apparently enjoyed a popularity of considerable duration since it ranked high in the 1991 memory of an alumnus of the Club who told me he had sung it as late as 1933.

Penn Glee Club at Irvine Auditorium – 1928
Used with permission – University Archives & Records Center – University of Pennsylvania

PENNSYLVANIA, HONORED MOTHER

It was often the case in the 19th century that students would put new lyrics to existing melodies and gain an "instant Penn song," of which this is a fine example. Whereas the wonderful Welsh song "Men of Harlech" (to which this set of lyrics was written) is still sung with great vigor to drum and trumpet accompaniment by the Penn Glee Club, these words by Thomas Blaine Donaldson, Class of 1899, don't get much play anymore.

PENNSYLVANIA, HONORED MOTHER

Words by
THOMAS BLAINE DONALDSON 1899

"MEN OF HARLECH"
WELSH FOLK SONG

a! Hail, with ad - mi - ra - tion!

Hail, with true e - la - tion! A song we raise. Thro'

end - less days We bring you loy - al - ty and ven - er - a - tion.

Al - ma Ma - ter! One! For - ev - er! Love and__ Faith no age shall sev - er,

Glo - ri - ous, tri - umph - ant ev - er, Penn - syl - va - ni - a!

NOW THANK WE ALL OUR GOD

Words by
MARTIN RINKART

Music by
JOHANN CRÜGER

bless - ed us on our way, With And count - less gifts of
guide us when per - plexed, And free us from all
earth and heav'n a - dore, For thus it was, is

love, And still is ours to - day. A - men.
ills In this world and the next.
now, And shall be ev - er - more.

NOW THANK WE ALL OUR GOD

There aren't many hymns in this book. However, this sturdy old one – with words written by Martin Rinkart in 1630 and music by Johann Crueger in 1647 – is included here because it was, for many years, closely identified with the University and was always sung at its chapel services and Commencement ceremonies.

A SONG FOR FATHER BEN

Words by
VINCENT B. BRECHT 1898

Music by
REGINALD DE KOVEN

be good sports-men eve - ry one As sons of Fa - ther Ben._____

scat - tered far and wide, my lads, We'll toast old Fa - ther Ben._____ 1-2. So

Piu mosso

sing, lads, and cheer, lads, with a heart for an - y fate._____ Through all____ our days we'll

sing the praise of Penn - syl - va - ni - a. Yes, sing, lads, and cheer, lads, with a

heart for an - y fate._____ Through all____ our days we'll sing the praise of

Penn - syl-van - i - a,_____ of Penn - syl-van - i - a._____

2. And_

A SONG FOR FATHER BEN

This is another example of the many songs written to existing melodies – a practice so prevalent in the 19th century. (It would be another dozen years before copyright laws frowned severely and put a real crimp on that sort of thing.) Vincent B. Brecht, Class of 1898, wrote his lyric to a rousing song "Brown October Ale" from Reginald DeKoven's popular 1891 operetta *Robin Hood*. At least the lyricists generally chose pretty good songs to adapt.

Toast throwing from upper tier at Franklin Field – 1988
Used with permission – University Archives & Records Center – University of Pennsylvania

PENN GLEE CLUB TOAST

The "Penn Glee Club Toast" is so uniquely the Glee Club's greeting that I make no pretense of arranging it for solo voice and piano for this book. It is included here only as originally written for *a cappella* male voices. At the time of this publication, it is probably the most frequently performed song in this book – sung at the drop of a hat by the Glee Club to greet any person or group it meets. While the club has sung it thousands of times in the U. S. and in dozens of countries throughout the world, perhaps my favorite rendition of all was when we were ushered, in hushed and reverent tones, into the crypt below the First Unitarian Church in Quincy, Massachusetts, to pay our respects to the side-by-side tombs of John Adams and John Quincy Adams. When asked if we would like to sing – our guides expecting, of course, something like "America the Beautiful" – the Club spontaneously burst forth with a lusty "Oh here's to the Adams', fill up the tankard . . . !"

PENN GLEE CLUB TOAST

Words and Music by
BRUCE MONTGOMERY

At this point, interpolate the name of the person, group or institution being toasted, such as "Pennsylvania"

VICTORIOUS PENNSYLVANIA

Words and Music by
J. RENTON HANEY 1910

Now they're off, they fight the line to sev- er, and they'll con - quer all our foes.____
Show them how our team can pull to-geth-er and win bat - tles as of yore.____

Chorus

L'istesso tempo

Penn - syl-va - nia staunch and true, And thy col - ors Red and Blue;

p, repeat f

Moth - er of our col - lege days, Days be-yond com - pare,____

Raise thy stan-dards to the sky; Let thy ban-ners wave on high; Spread thy glo - ry

o'er the land, Oh, Al-ma Ma-ter ev - er fair._____ fair._____

VICTORIOUS PENNSYLVANIA

J. Renton "Rent" Haney wrote the words and music of this march while he was the undergraduate leader of the Glee Club. In a 1960 letter, Haney referred to this song as "sung on the football field and also sung in harmony by the Glee Club, but I suppose it is long since dead." Well, as a matter of fact, Rent, I regret to say it is! Perhaps this volume will resurrect it?

Penn Glee Club feeling victorious at Macy's Thanksgiving Day Parade – 1970's
Used with permission – Penn Glee Club

48

MEMORIES

Words by
P.C. STUART 1897

Music by
WILLIAM J. GOECKEL 1896

1. When peace - ful twi - light draw - eth near, When toil and care are
2. When Au - tumn brings her with - ered leaves, And mea - dows brown and

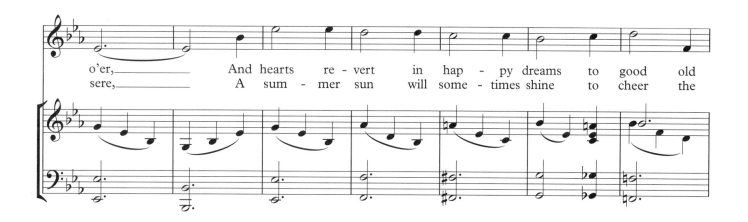

o'er,_____ And hearts re - vert in hap - py dreams to good old
sere,_____ A sum - mer sun will some - times shine to cheer the

days of yore,_____ We drink of mem - 'ry's sweet - est
dy - ing year,_____ So in the fall of life will

cup and drink__ it oft a - gain__ When dream - ing of our
come, when we__ are gray - haired men__ A joy in dream - ing

col - lege days, The days__ at dear__ old Penn.__
of the days, Our days__ at dear__ old Penn.__

Refrain **Tempo di Waltz**

Dear old Penn,_____ dear old Penn,_____ how sweet - ly come to our

MEMORIES

This was once a very popular song on campus. Composed by William J. Goeckel when he was the undergraduate leader of the Glee Club, it doesn't display the originality or lasting quality of his still very popular "The Red and Blue." Still, five hundred is a pretty decent batting average.

ALMA MATER

Words by
ISAAC HAMPSHUR JONES 1906

Music by
L. V. H. CROSBY

Old Al - ma Ma - ter, great and grand, Re-nown'd from sea to sea, Wher-e'er thy loy - al
Dear Penn, tho' spa-cious be thy halls, And wide thy cam-pus spread, And tho' thy ad - a-

sons shall stand, They'll e'er be true to thee. The sight of thy maj - es - tic halls, With
-man - tine walls Tall, tow - er o - ver - head, Yet all too nar - row are thy bounds Our

i - vy o - ver - grown, The fond-est mem - o - ry re - calls That we have ev - er known.
feal - ty to con - tain For hark! the ve - ry sky re-sounds And ech - oes our re - frain.

Chorus
Melody in 2nd Tenor

ff Old Penn - syl - va - ni - a_____ Dear Penn - syl - va - ni - a,_____ We'll

e'er be true to Red and Blue Of Penn - syl - va - ni - a._____

ALMA MATER

The title of this song is misleading in that it never was Penn's alma mater. The words were written by Isaac Hampshur Jones when he was the undergraduate leader of the Glee Club in 1906. He wrote them to a tune that had been sung by the Club since its very beginning and, indeed, was featured on the program of the very first Glee Club public performance. The original heart-rending ballad, "The Last Cigar" tells the sad tale of a man on board a ship "off the blue Canary Isles" who realizes, to his dismay, that he is smoking his last cigar with no chance of getting ashore to replenish his supply. You smokers know that feeling, don't you? You've shared his plaintive cry "I watched the ashes as it came fast drawing to the end; I watched it as a friend would watch beside a dying friend." Young Mr. Jones obviously liked the rich male choral harmonies of the song and decided that they should live on in a far loftier setting.

53

DRINK A HIGHBALL

      Probably no Penn song has been so clouded in mystery over the years as to its origin, or embroiled in so much controversy as to its ownership, as "Drink a Highball." It seems to have appeared first as "The Glorious Highball" in a popular Broadway show entitled *The Isle of Spice*, written in 1904 by Gus Brigham of Chicago and dedicated to Herbert Watrous. T. H. "Monty" Montgomery (not a relation as far as I know), Wesleyan University Class of 1902, acquired the right from Watrous to adapt it as a song for Wesleyan. The song was then brought to Pennsylvania by two Wesleyan transfer students: Reginald H. Stow, 1908 Dental, and W. "Ray" Bristol, 1909 Architecture. The song became so popular at Penn that students at Wesleyan were accused of borrowing or actually stealing it from the Quakers! In a November 1, 1940 letter, Stow wrote: "Ray Bristol and I did teach the song to the Penn boys, and I well remember the difficulty we had in changing the words around so it would sound right for Penn . . . I really think both colleges made a mountain out of a molehill in the controversy that has been going on since 1906. I have never regretted carrying the song to Penn especially when I realize how much real pleasure the Penn boys have had in its use." To add to the mystery, I have a 1960 letter from J. Renton Haney, Class of 1910, claiming that he and class-mate Rod Merrick were the ones who "stole the old Wesleyan song . . . and brought it back" to Penn. There appears to be no way to verify this and the Stow-Bristol explanation is the one most widely accepted. Dr. George E. Nitzsche, Class of 1898 and one of the great musicologists and historians of his day, uncovered an even greater mystery when he wrote that he was inclined to believe that the song was not original with anyone in America. "What convinced me that our beautiful 'Drink a Highball' song was not original with anyone in Chicago, Wesleyan or Pennsylvania," he wrote in Franklin Field Illustrated (October 19, 1940, Vol. 25, No. 3), is the fact that a year before the World War [WW I] I was entertaining Major McGrail, of the British Army, who had served in the Boer War. One afternoon, on Franklin Field, when the cheering section was singing the High Ball Song, the Major, who had recently arrived from England, sang the song with great gusto. Greatly surprised, I asked him, 'Where did you get that song, Major?' 'Oh,' he replied, 'That is one of our old barrack songs – we used to sing it in South Africa.'" So, when you come right down to it, "Drink a Highball" may well be entangled in the intrigue of international theft and plagiarism well antedating Broadway, Wesleyan, Pennsylvania, or any other group currently laying claim to it. Whatever the origin, it's one of Penn's most beloved songs and is sung worldwide by students and alumni alike. Its identity with Penn is almost universally acknowledged. So there!

DRINK A HIGHBALL

Adapted from Words and Music by
G.B. BRIGHAM

Drink a high-ball at night-fall, be good fel-lows while you may. For to-mor-row may bring sor-row, so to-night let's all be gay. Tell the sto-ry of glo-ry of Penn-syl-va-ni-a. Drink a high-ball and be jol-ly! Here's a toast to dear old Penn.

THREE CHEERS FOR THE RED AND THE BLUE

Words by
FREDERICK B. NIELSON 1890

Music variously attributed

Maestoso

Solo

Penn - syl - va - nia, the gem of cre - a - tion,__ The strong and the brave__ and the

true:__ No won - der, in proud ad - mi - ra - tion,__ De -

vot - ed - ly our hearts__ beat for you. 'Tis well that all foes__ should__

trem - ble,__ When__ met, Penn - syl - va - nia dear, by you! Should the

THREE CHEERS FOR THE RED AND THE BLUE

Frederick B. Neilson, Class of 1890, did more than just "adapt" his lyric to the familiar tune "Columbia, the Gem of the Ocean" – also known as "Three Cheers For the Red, White and Blue" (which is the way the music is identified in the Penn songbooks of 1903 to 1923). His words are a virtual parody of the original with relatively minor changes to make them less militant and more idealistic. But what I find most intriguing about the song is deciding to whom the credit should go for the composition of the music. When the song was first published, in Philadelphia in 1843, under the title "Columbia, the Land of the Brave" – with words and music credited to David T. Shaw – Stephen Meany, an English journalist, objected that he had written virtually the same lyric a year earlier as "Britannia, the Pride of the Ocean" to exactly the same tune composed by his friend Thomas Williams. But a few weeks after the Philadelphia publication, yet another song came out as "Columbia, the Gem of the Ocean" allegedly by one Thomas A. Becket! Becket claimed that he and Shaw had collaborated on the song, well before its publication, for Shaw's singing act at a Philadelphia theater. I guess we'll never know for certain but I think I've been eminently fair by mentioning all three possible composers.

Cheerleaders at Franklin Field
Used with permission – The *Record*, Penn Year Book – 1955

RAH! RAH! FOR PENN

This rather trite song is remarkable mostly because its music was composed by Frederic R. Mann, Class of 1924. Mann went on to become one of the great benefactors of the University and of music in general with musical edifices bearing his distinguished name both in the United States and Israel. I guess one has to start somewhere!

RAH! RAH! FOR PENN

Words by
EDWARDS S. DUNN 1887

Music by
FREDERIC R. MANN 1924

Dr. Clay Boland writing and arranging music – 1926
Used with permission – Mask and Wig

OLD PENNSYLVANIA

Clay Boland and Frank Winegar, both of the Class of 1926, wrote the words and music to this song. Boland is best known for the many songs he composed for the Mask & Wig Club in the 1920's and '30's (usually to lyrics by Moses "Moe" Jaffe, Wharton 1923, Law 1927). Their tunes gained considerable popularity nationwide through recordings by some of the top swing bands of the day.

OLD PENNSYLVANIA

Words and music by
CLAY BOLAND 1926
and FRANK WINEGAR 1926

not with - out the men, who lend their help with song and cheers.
don't for - get — you sure can bet, we're with you — to the man.

Chorus

Old Penn-syl - va - nia!_____ My Penn-syl - va - nia!_____ Keep right a -

- head, where you be - long,_____ Don't dis-ap - point this loy - al

throng,_____ We are here, ten thou - sand strong,_____ Just to re -

-mind you____ We're right be - hind you____ With one ap - peal— let them

feel your might____ So Penn-syl - va - nia,____ Let us pro -

-claim you,____ As the one who'll win this

1.
fight.

2.
Old Penn - syl - fight.____

D.S.

fz D.S.

BEN BOLT

Words by
THOMAS DUNN ENGLISH 1839

Music by
NELSON KNEASS

BEN BOLT

Another song included for its historical significance is "Ben Bolt," an extremely popular song of the mid-19th century. It was never considered a Penn song but has been included in all of the previously-published collections of our University's music because of the authorship of the lyric. With words written by Thomas Dunn English of the Class of 1839, and music by Nelson Kneass, "Ben Bolt" was sung at Penn and swept the country in music halls and theaters throughout the United States.

John Philip Sousa conducting Penn Band in the student triangle – November 21, 1930
Used with permission – University Archives & Records Center – University of Pennsylvania

AVE, PENNSYLVANIA

There are numerous songs in this volume that no longer enjoy continuing popularity among students or even alumni. Some have dropped out of favor because they aren't especially memorable. Some are dated, by references to events or situations that now seem a little too remote or precious for today's tastes. But a number of them are so appropriate to their time and place in Penn's history and traditions that any representative record of these traditions must include them. "Ave, Pennsylvania" obviously was written as a reflection on World War I; its idealism of pen-over-sword is illustrative of the sentiments of that time. It appears here, however, for two additional reasons. It happens to be a perfectly beautiful song – so much so that the Glee Club has chosen to include it in three recordings of Penn songs. It also has the added virtue of boasting a lyric penned by S. Weir Mitchell, a prominent physician, poet and man of letters, who remains one of Penn's all-time distinguished alumni; and music by Hugh A. Clarke, for many years a member of our University's music faculty and longtime director of the Glee Club.

AVE PENNSYLVANIA

Words by
S. WEIR MITCHELL 1848

Music by
HUGH A. CLARKE

Ma - ter A - ma - ta, moth - er a - dored Of
Lau - rels un - fad - ing for - ev - er are thine, But

men who were no - ble by pen and by sword, The earth and the
fresh are the ro - ses we lov - ing - ly twine;___ Ma - ter di -

o - cean have tak - en thy sons, Where flut - tered___ the___
-lec - ta,___ lo! from a - bove Heav - en___ smiles___

star - flag and thun - dered the guns. 2. Tho'
down on thee, take___ thou our love.

WE GATHER HERE

Words by
EDWARD F. KENNEY 1887

GERMAN FOLK SONG

1. We gath-er here, from year to year, For good old Penn-syl-va-ni-a! Her
2. She's push-ing on, still push-ing on, Our dear old Penn-syl-va-ni-a! Her

fu-ture bless, her past to cheer, Our good old Penn-syl-va-ni-a! When
prog-ress one tri-um-phant song For dear old Penn-syl-va-ni-a! The

e'er we see the Red and Blue, Sym-bol-i-cal of all that's true, We'll
pride of ev-'ry stal-wart son, Who sees her lau-rels fair-ly won, Her

then our loy-al-ty re-new, For good old Penn-syl-va-ni-a!
march of vic-to-ry be-gun For dear old Penn-syl-va-ni-a!

WE GATHER HERE

Here is another lyric set to a familiar tune. While it appeared in the 1903 songbook without any mention of where the tune came from, it was attributed to the song "Maryland, My Maryland" in the 1909 and subsequent editions. In point of fact, the Christmas song "O Tannenbaum, O Tannenbaum" is the real tune source and it's a good deal older than "Maryland, My Maryland." No one knows who composed its music but it is universally accepted as an old German folk tune.

Penn Glee Club at Ben Franklin statue in front of College Hall – 1960's
Used with permission – Penn Glee Club

BEN FRANKLIN, ESQ.

I have already noted that a number of songs included here are no longer in general use. Still, some are valid reminders of our past and occasionally prove to be just the right thing to resurrect for special occasions. "Ben Franklin, Esq." is a perfect example of this genre. Today we consider it passé and corny. But in January 1990, with the First City Troop mounted on horseback and wearing full colonial regalia, with president Sheldon Hackney and a professional impersonator of Benjamin Franklin arriving on College Hall Green in an open carriage to fanfares played on long heraldic trumpets, it proved the ideal song for the Glee Club to sing to begin the University's year-long celebration of its 250th birthday.

BEN FRANKLIN, ESQ.

Words by
CHARLES I. JUNKIN 1877

Music by
EDWARD G. McCOLLIN 1878

Fast, with vigor and snap ... *Slower*

H' - rah! H' - rah! H' - rah! Penn - syl - va - ni - a!

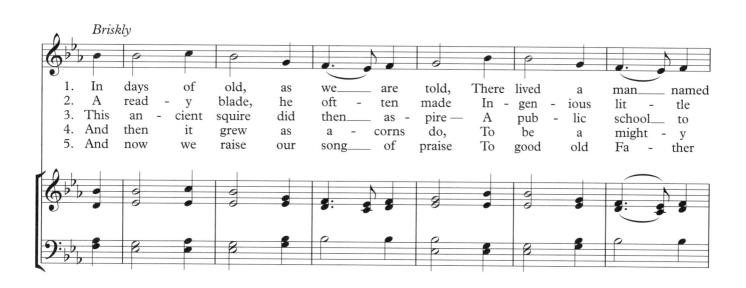

Briskly

1. In days of old, as we___ are told, There lived a man___ named
2. A read - y blade, he oft - ten made In - gen - ious lit - tle
3. This an - cient squire did then___ as - pire — A pub - lic school___ to
4. And then it grew as a - corns do, To be a might - y
5. And now we raise our song___ of praise To good old Fa - ther

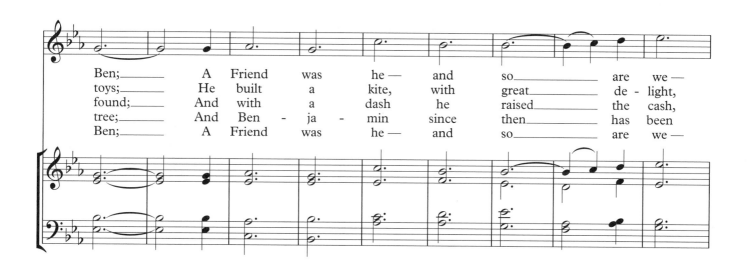

Ben;___ A Friend was he — and so___ are we —
toys;___ He built a kite, with great___ de - light,
found;___ And with a dash he raised___ the cash,
tree;___ And Ben - ja - min since then___ has been
Ben;___ A Friend was he — and so___ are we —

OUR BOYS IN RED AND BLUE

Words by
CLAYTON F. McMICHAEL 1891

Composer Unknown

Is it strange when the boys start play-ing,_____ That our eyes fill up with tears,_____ As they run, and smash, and tum - ble,_____ And the stands ring out the cheers?_____ For it's then that our heart re - joi - ces_____ In a

OUR BOYS IN RED AND BLUE

The historical significance of this seldom-revived song is the fact that the lyric was written – to the tune of an old ditty "Her Boy In Blue" – by Clayton Fotterall McMichael, Class of 1891. McMichael was one of the founders of the Mask & Wig Club in 1889. I have made every possible attempt to acknowledge the composer of the old melody but, even with diligent research by the music staff of the Library of Congress, I have been unsuccessful in identifying the original song. Almost certainly it was a song of the Civil War and referred to a soldier from the North.

GAUDEAMUS IGITUR

Authorship unknown

Old German Student Song
Arranged by BRUCE MONTGOMERY

Majestic, but not too slow

f -pp

1. Gau - de - a - mus i - gi - tur, ju - ve - nes dum su - mus.
2. Vi - vat a - ca - de - mi - a, vi - vant pro - fes - sor - es.

mf

Post ju - cun - dam ju - ven - tu - tem, post mo - les - tam sen - ec - tu - tem, nos ha - be - bit____
Vi - vat mem-brum quod - li - bet, vi - vant mem-bra quae - li - bet, sem-per sint in____

1.

D.C. 2. *rit.*

hu - mus, nos ha-be - bit____ hu - mus.
flo - re, sem-per sint in____ flo - re.

rit.

GAUDEAMUS IGITUR

This is perhaps the best known student song ever written. The words and music, both of unknown authorship, were composed about the year 1267. It has been sung for more than seven hundred years by students throughout the world and for more than 200 years at Penn. In his operetta *The Student Prince*, Sigmund Romberg lends verisimilitude to his score by having the Heidelberg students sing "Gaudeamus Igitur." It is the sweeping finale of Brahms' "Academic Festival Overture," a work based on the great German student songs. When the Penn Glee Club was touring the Soviet Union (now, of course, Russia) in 1971, we were hosted in Leningrad (now St. Petersburg) by a Russian male chorus. Each chorus sang its own repertoire and when the time came to sing something jointly, the natural first suggestion was "Gaudeamus Igitur."

PENN GLEE CLUB MARCH (PENNy-WHISTLE)

To commemorate the 125th Anniversary of the Penn Glee Club - 1987

BRUCE MONTGOMERY

Trio (*The melody line of the Trio is whistled. Thus, the subtitle!*)

Whistling Chorus

78

PENN GLEE CLUB MARCH (PENN-y WHISTLE)

With the Penn Glee Club's impending 125th anniversary in 1987 it occurred to me that, while a lot of people had written songs for the Glee Club to sing, no one had ever composed a work to specifically honor the group itself. I had written a musical for the Penn Players in 1967 entitled *Why Me?* It had a pretty good march in it that I thought was worth reviving and extending beyond the life of the show. With some major rewriting to make it more accessible for general use, I orchestrated it for full band and had the trio of the march (which later works in counterpoint with the first theme) whistled, so that almost anyone could perform it without requiring a trained glee club to pull it off! The Penn Band – with the Glee Club whistling – premiered the march at the Yale-Pennsylvania Homecoming football game in Franklin Field on October 25, 1986, to kick off the Club's anniversary season. I had the pleasure of conducting it on that occasion.

HAIL, COLUMBIA

Another historical inclusion, "Hail, Columbia" was written by Joseph Hopkinson, Class of 1786 (son of Francis Hopkinson), to the tune of the "President's March," and was part of the Glee Club repertoire for many years. The song played an important role when the young country was on the brink of war with France during the presidency of John Adams. The Federalists favored England while the Republicans, led by Thomas Jefferson, sided with France. Congress bitterly debated the issue during the summer of 1798. At the urging of a young actor named Gilbert Fox, Hopkinson wrote lyrics which extolled America and discreetly omitted any mention of either England or France. It was an immediate hit with both parties and became so well known and popular that it was given serious consideration at one time to become our National Anthem.

HAIL, COLUMBIA

Words by
JOSEPH HOPKINSON 1796

Music by
PHILIP PHILE

1. Hail, Co - lum - bia, hap - py land! Hail, ye he - roes!
2. Im - mor - tal pa - triots! rise once more, De - fend your rights; de -
3. Sound,___ sound the trump of fame! Let___ Wash - ing -
4. Be - hold the Chief who now com - mands, Once more to serve his

heaven - born band! Who fought and bled in Free - dom's___cause, Who fought and bled in
-fend your shore: Let no rude foe, with im - pious___hand, Let no rude foe, with
-ton's great name Ring through the world with loud___ ap - plause, Ring through the world with
coun - try stands. The rock on which the storm___ will___beat; The rock on which the

Free - dom's___ cause, And when the storm of war was gone, En -
im - pious___ hand, In - vade the shrine where sa - cred lies, Of
loud___ ap - plause, Let ev - 'ry chime to free - dom dear,___
storm___ will___ beat; But armed in vir - tue, firm and true, His

- joyed___ the___ peace your val - or won. Let
toil___ and___ blood the well - earned prize. While
Lis - ten___ with a joy - ful ear. With
hopes___ are___ fixed on heav'n and you. When

in - de - pen - dence be___ our___ boast, Ev - er mind - ful
of - f'ring peace, sin - cere___ and___ just, In heav'n we place a
e - qual skill with god - like___ pow'r, He gov - erns in the
hope was sink - ing in___ dis - may, When gloom ob - scured Co -

what it cost; Ev - er grate - ful for the prize Let its al - tar
man - ly trust, That truth and just - tice will pre - vail, And ev - 'ry scheme of
fear - ful hour Of hor - rid war; or guides with ease The hap - pier times of
- lum - bia's day, His stead - y mind from chan - ges free, Re - solved on death or

reach the skies.
bond - age fail.
hon - est peace. Firm, u - ni - ted, let us be, Rally - ing round our
Lib - er - ty.

lib - er - ty; As a band of broth - ers joined, Peace and safe - ty we shall find.

THE BOWL FIGHT

Words by
W. L. ROWLAND, 1878

Music by
ZÖLLNER

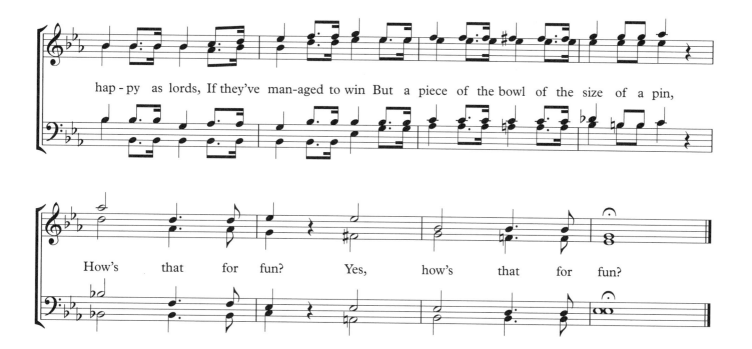

hap - py as lords, If they've man-aged to win But a piece of the bowl of the size of a pin,

How's that for fun? Yes, how's that for fun?

THE BOWL FIGHT

At the end of the first term each year at the University of Pennsylvania, it was the custom for sophomores to attempt to fit the freshman who had the lowest grades for the term into a large wooden bowl. If the sophomores succeeded in cramming him in, the bowl became his. If they failed, the freshman class tried to smash the bowl and divide the pieces. Old photographs portray the game as muddy mayhem! In modern times, the bowl is given as an award to one of the four senior Honor Men – and the melee that originally earned its name has been relegated to footnotes of history such as this.

Freshmen fighting with Sophomores to stay out of the bowl – 1920's
Used with permission – University Archives & Records Center – University of Pennsylvania

"The Quakerettes" – 1964
Used with permission – Penn Band Archives

THE SONGS OF PENNSYLVANIA ⟿

This is yet another Penn song set to the tune of "John Brown's Body." [See the notes for "The Field Cry of Penn" for more information on this melody.] The words are by Arthur Hobson Quinn, Class of 1894, who became a distinguished and longtime member of Penn's English Department faculty. One of his better-known contributions to the University was his daughter, Kathleen Carberry Quinn, who founded the co-ed student theatre troupe, The Pennsylvania Players, in 1936 and directed them until her retirement in 1964.

THE SONGS OF PENNSYLVANIA

Words by
ARTHUR HOBSON QUINN 1894

Music by
WILLIAM STEFFE

Allegretto

1. Sing a song of glo - ry, boys, and make it loud and strong,
2. Through - out all our col - lege life we've sung these songs of Penn,
3. Ev - 'ry loy - al son of Penn has sung them just the same,

Sing it as we used to sing it while we marched a - long;
Sung them for her col - ors and her maid - ens and her men;
Sung them through de - feat and doubt un - til her tri - umph came;

Let the dear and hon - ored name be ev - er in your song of Penn - syl - va - nia - a.
We will sing the cho - rus till the ech - oes ring a - gain for Penn - syl - va - nia - a.
Sung them till the ci - ty streets were ring - ing with the name of Penn - syl - va - nia - a.

Full Chorus

Penn - syl, Penn - syl, Penn - syl - va - nia, Penn - syl, Penn - syl, Penn - syl - va_____ nia;

Penn - syl, Penn - syl, Penn - syl - va - nia, Penn - syl - va - ni - a.

UNIVERSITY OF PENNSYLVANIA HYMN

Music ascribed to
JOHN FRANCIS WADE
Adapted by
EDWARD G. McCOLLIN 1878

Words by
THOMAS WISTAR 1863

UNIVERSITY OF PENNSYLVANIA HYMN

With a lyric by Thomas Wistar, Class of 1863, this hymn was adapted by Edward G. McCollin, Class of 1878, to the familiar Christmas carol, "Adeste Fideles." While the carol was probably based on a much older tune, the melody – as now known – is generally ascribed to John Francis Wade (1711-1786) and first was published in his *Cantus Diversi* in 1751. As Pennsylvania's hymn, it was sung regularly in University chapel services during the latter part of the 19th and into the 20th centuries.

CAMPUS AND HALL

Words by
THOMAS B. DONALDSON 1899

Music by
CHARLES GILPIN III 1899

1. "Come, all ye loy - al class - men now," and ral - ly a - gain for our old Fa - ther Ben in the land of old Penn. And bring a stein and pipe a - long, we'll fill up with cheer, sing - ing Penn - syl - va - nia

2. all the years to come you'll find the fair i - vy vine, like old friends and old wine, 'round our heart will en - twine. For us but one fra - ter - ni - ty, the true "Red and Blue," bind - ing to e - ter - ni -

songs._____ Out for Al - ma Ma - ter with a song or bat - tle -
ty._____ Al - ways best "In East or West," the Penn - syl - va - nia

cry, And vie - ing with the ech - oes from the sky!_____
maid; Her mem - o - ry will nev - er, nev - er fade._____

Ev - er march - ing on for Penn - syl - va - - nia, while her
So we sing of her and Penn - syl - va - - nia, with the

pen - nant we float on high. Rah!
old crowd on dress pa - rade. Rah!

CAMPUS AND HALL

Subtitled "A Song-Medley", this charming ditty borrows from a number of songs popular on campus at the time that Thomas L. Donaldson and Charles Gilpin III, both of the Class of 1899, wrote it for a 1909 Mask & Wig production entitled *Merely a Monarch*. The songs that are subtly quoted in the medley include "The Red and Blue," "Hang Jeff Davis," "Mary Had a Little Lamb" and "How Dry I Am."

The Penn Band on field – Circa 1986
Used with permission – Penn Band

PENN – PENN – PENN

Written in 1909, this song elicits two personal observations. First, the verse, while probably an innocent coincidence, starts out almost note-for-note with the melody of "The Magnet and the Churn" from Gilbert & Sullivan's *Patience*. And second, there is an arrangement of this march in the library of the Penn Band that was performed by onetime director Bruce C. Beach under a completely different title: "Fight, Penn, Fight!" When or why the title was changed – or by whom – remains a minor mystery.

PENN - PENN - PENN

Words by
J. DAWSON PAUL 1910

Music by
RUSSELL S. BOLES 1912

Blue. Come, ye loy - al sons of Penn - syl - va - nia, And loud - ly cheer our team a -

- gain,_____ For they'll ne'er give in, But they'll

Rah, rah, rah, rah. rah, rah.
fight to win for Penn, Penn, Penn. 2. Fight Penn.

97

WITH JEMMY ON THE SEA ♪

As stated in the introduction to this volume, Francis Hopkinson, Class of 1757, is generally recognized as America's first native-born composer of consequence. After his graduation from Penn, Hopkinson wrote several choral works for the University's Commencements. The earliest that I have discovered was in 1760. This, and others, prompted Edward Potts Cheyney, in his *History of the University of Pennsylvania 1740-1940*, to state that "this gifted young man . . . gave to the early Commencements of the College a musical significance unique among American colonial colleges." While "With Jemmy On the Sea" is not strictly a Penn song, it is one that has been used for its historical significance several times during my years at Penn. I even employed it, performed by two singers with harpsichord and flute accompaniment, in a film produced by the University in the 1960's. The song was originally one of a collection of eight songs by Hopkinson, published in 1788 and dedicated to his friend George Washington. In the version included in this songbook, I have been faithful to the original and its rather stark simplicity. The only significant changes I have made are to the 18th century conventions concerning grace notes. While a singer of the period knew the traditions of their interpretation, today's singer (unless steeped in the music of that period) does not. Therefore, I have substituted true-value notes for these conventions. In the previously published versions of the song, there were confusing indications of repeats and final phrase endings. These, too, have been clarified and standardized.

WITH JEMMY ON THE SEA

Words and Music by
FRANCIS HOPKINSON 1757

99

swore,__ I__ blush'd and soon com - plied,____ I__ blush'd and soon com - plied,____ My
shore;__ I__ wiped my tears a - way,____ I__ wiped my tears a - way____ And
me;__ My__ anx - ious thoughts are toss'd____ My__ anx - ious thoughts are toss'd____ With

heart was his__ be - fore.__ My heart was his.____ My heart was his__ be__
saw his ship__ no__ more.__ No more, no more,__ And saw his ship no__
Jem - my on the__ sea.____ My thoughts are tossed With Jem - my on__ the__

fore._____
more._____
sea._____

One____
When__

1.2.   3.

JOHNNIE CROUSE

Traditional

Air: *"Auld Lang Syne"*

Melody in 2nd Tenor

Oh, John - nie Crouse He caught a mouse, And tied it to a string;

He__ took it to the riv - er-side, And__ there he chucked it in.

Now the lit - tle mouse He swam a-cross And sat up-on a stone;

Said the lit - tle mouse To John - nie Crouse, "See__ now what you have done."

JOHNNIE CROUSE

This quaint little ditty about a swimming mouse would hardly make it on its own into any serious collection of songs. It's here because it happens to be one of Penn's oldest songs. Set to the tune of "Auld Lang Syne," it was one of the rare songs from the dawn of the University that was not written in Latin.

Penn Glee Club snowball fight in white tie and tails – Wisconsin tour – 1979
Used with permission – Penn Glee Club

COLLEGE DAYS

Hugh A. Clarke was the first – and longtime – professional director of the Penn Glee Club. A member of the Music Department faculty, he composed and arranged a number of songs for the then-young group. The thing that strikes me most about this song is its parallel to "Afterglow," a tune of mine that has become a standard of the Glee Club. When I wrote the song I was not aware of "College Days" but I am struck that both works appeal even more to alumni "coming home" to the campus than to the students who sing it.

COLLEGE DAYS

Words by
CHARLES I. JUNKIN 1877

Music by
HUGH A. CLARKE

Youth, like a rose - bud, blooms but a day,___ Haste! for its beau - ty

Youth, like a rose-bud, blooms___ but a day,___

glid - eth a - way.

1. Sing of the broth - er - hood,
2. What, though the sky be not

strong and ten - der;
al - ways glow - ing!
Sing of thy loves in a gen - tler strain;
What, though the storm - clouds in - ter - vene!

Sing of the days___ re - plete with pleas - sure;
Youth has an eye that can pierce the dark - ness

Sing!___ for the mor - row may bring thee___ pain.
Catch - ing a glimpse of its cur - tained___ sheen.

THE PENNSYLVANIA FLYER

Words by
WILLIAM O. MILLER 1904

Music by
HEDDA VAN DEN BEEMT

Here comes the Penn-Penn-Penn-syl-va-nia Fly-er,_ Clear the track, for she has the right of way;

(2 whistles)

See her gal-lant crew In the Red and Blue, And they're head-ing straight for Vic-to-ry to-day. Ray! Ray!

shouting

Throw her throt-tle wide Till she hits her stride, In the good old fash-ioned way. So

shouting

(Cornell)* Stop! Look! And lis-ten! Or the folks will

* Name of opponent

find   you mis‑sin', When you   cross the track of Penn‑syl‑van‑i‑a.

THE PENNSYLVANIA FLYER

The music for this song was composed by Hedda Van den Beemt, a violinist with the Philadelphia Orchestra who was also a local teacher, conductor and – most likely – a colleague of Adolph Vogel, director of the Penn Band during its earliest days. The words are by William Otto Miller, Class of 1904, to whom all of us who make music at Penn are deeply indebted. He was responsible for bringing together, under one cover, the many songs of the University for their publication in 1903. The students would shout the then popular "Locomotive Cheer" at the conclusion of which this refrain was sung. "Flyer" was a common term of the day for a railroad train. The cheer – now long out of use – emulated the progressive speed of an old fashioned steam engine starting up and went as follows:

Rah – Rah – Rah – Rah (very slow)

        Penn – syl‑ van – ia

        Rah – Rah – Rah – Rah (slow)

        Penn – syl – van – ia

        Rah – Rah – Rah – Rah (faster)

        Penn – syl – van – ia

        Rah – Rah – Rah – Rah (still faster)

        Penn – syl – van – ia!

        Ray_____!

Penn Glee Club in Concert – 1960's
Used with permission – Penn Glee Club

PENNSYLVANIA! PENNSYLVANIA!

Thornton Oakley, Class of 1901, was one of the most revered teachers, authors and artists of the University whose fame stretched far beyond campus boundaries. Robert Elmore, Class of 1937, was the accompanist for the Glee Club during his undergraduate years at Penn. He then went on to become an internationally renowned organist, teacher and composer. "Pennsylvania! Pennsylvania!" – written by the pair – was one of the numerous songs composed to celebrate Penn's bicentennial in 1940 and was published that year in a modest collection of songs called *Bicentennial Songs*. I was amused when I first saw this song because it fairly cries out that it was composed by an organist. The music for the left hand was undoubtedly played on the organ pedals with the composer's nimble musical feet.

PENNSYLVANIA! PENNSYLVANIA!

Words by
THORTON OAKLEY 1901

Music by
ROBERT ELMORE 1937

Monty rehearsing mixed chorus of Penn students
Used with permission – Bruce Montgomery Foundation for the Arts

ACADEMIC FESTIVE ANTHEM

This work was commissioned for the May 14, 1990 Commencement in celebration of the University of Pennsylvania's 250th anniversary. It was performed by the Commencement Chorus and the First United States Army Band at graduation exercises in Franklin Field and was conducted by the composer. The music is set to words by Benjamin Franklin, taken from his "Proposals Relating to the Education of Youth in Pennsylvania." I never anticipated that it would become the "standard" anthem for many Commencements and official ceremonies thereafter, including the inauguration of Judith Rodin, with organ accompaniment, as President of the University on October 21, 1994.

ACADEMIC FESTIVE ANTHEM

Words by
BENJAMIN FRANKLIN

Music by
BRUCE MONTGOMERY

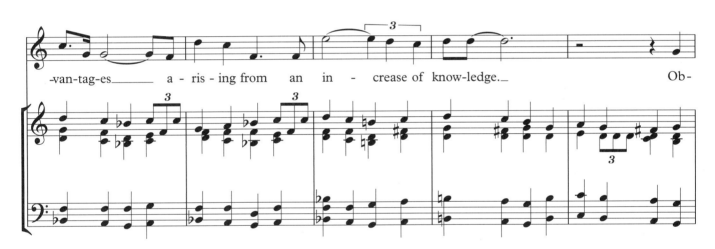

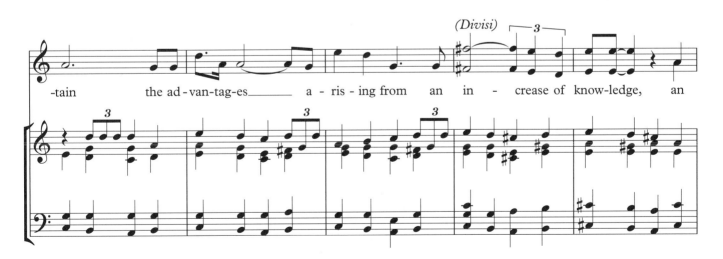

111

in-crease of know-ledge. And pre-vent,___ as much as may be, The mis-chiev-ious con-se-quen-ces

that would at-tend a gen-er-al ig-nor-ance a - mong us.___

Learn ev-ery-thing that is use-ful And ev-ery-

dim.

112

-thing＿＿ that is or-na-men-tal.

But art is long and time is

short.

There-fore,

learn those things that are like-ly to be

Most use-ful＿＿ and most or-na-men-tal.＿＿

Fix in the minds of youth, Fix in the minds of youth Deep im-press-ions of the beau-ty,___ The

beau-ty___ and use-ful-ness, The beau-ty and use-ful - ness_____ of vir - tue.___

Tempo I

True mer-it con-sists in an in - cli-na-tion

Tempo I

Joined with an a-bil-i-ty to serve man-kind.

poco allargando

Which a - bil - i - ty   is (with the bless-ing of God)_ to be ac - quired, Or great-ly   in -

-creased____ by true learn-ing,_   And should,   in-deed, be the great aim   and

end   of   all____   learn - ing._____

GOOD-NIGHT

Words by
HARRY C. WESTERVELT

Music by
R. L. DePEARSALL

Moderato (♩ = 112)

f 1. And now, a - las! 'tis time to part, Good-night to all, good-night; May
mf 2. To Penn - syl - va - nia's friends so true, We say good-night, good-night; To

joy and peace dwell in each heart, Good-night to all, good-night. For
all who love the Red and Blue We say good-night, good-night. May

we must go ere day doth break And morn - ing come with
glad - ness all your mo - ments fill As on through life you

cresc.

1.
f glad - some light, And so we say to all, good-night, We say to all, good-night. *rall.*

2.
cresc. go, And may sweet mem-'ries lin - ger still, When we have said good - night, And *ff*

may sweet mem -'ries lin - ger still, When we have said good - night. Good -

night, good-night, good-night, good - night, good - night, good - night.

good- night, good - night,

GOOD-NIGHT

The lyric for this overly sentimental song was written by Harry E. Westervelt, the same student who teamed up on "The Red and Blue" with infinitely greater success. It was edited and adapted to R. L. DePearsall's music by William Stansfield, who received his music degree from Penn in 1902.

FIGHT FOR PENN

Written in 1907 when lyricist Norman L. Harker was a junior, the music for this song was composed by Paul Eno, at that time the director of the Combined Musical Clubs. During the last decade of the 19th century and the first of the 20th, almost every sentimental song written about the University was published in sheet music form and found its way to parlor pianos in most respectable homes. This is one of the few "fight songs" that was also accorded this honor. Until the 1923 edition of the songbook was published, previous editions had listed it under the title "Fight for Penn." For reasons unexplained, it appears in the 1923 volume as "Fight for Pennsylvania." On Alumni Day, May 15, 1993, however, I had a delightful chat with alumnus Marvin Weiner who presented me with a photocopy of the original sheet music which unmistakably bore the title "Fight for Penn." As a result, I have changed the title in the Table of Contents, the Background Notes and on the song itself and restored it to its correct title – with thanks to Mr. Weiner.

FIGHT FOR PENN

Words by
NORMAN L. HARKER 1908

Music by
PAUL ENO

fray,   we will win a - gain,_____ While for her   our   shouts   and   cheers re - cur,_____
yield,   firm we'll ev - er be,_____ And we'll fight   to   win   thee   fame and praise,_____
so,   Fight our men so bold,_____ Nev - er lose   nor   fear   de - feat to - day_____

___ For vic - to - ry, (Hoorah, Hoorah,)_____ e - ter - nal - ly, (Hoorah, Hoorah,)_____ For dear old
___ Thy col - ors   true, (Hoorah, Hoorah,)_____ old Red and   Blue, (Hoorah, Hoorah,)_____ Shall stand for
___ The fight is   done, (Hoorah, Hoorah,)_____ the game is   won, (Hoorah, Hoorah,)_____ For dear old

Chorus

Penn - syl - va - ni - a._____
Penn and vic - to - ry._____   Fight for Penn - syl - va - ni - a,_____
Penn - syl - va - ni - a._____

___ Fight for Penn, boys,   for we must win to - day,_____   So   stand true, and

(Hoorah! Hoorah!)

fight for Red and Blue, For the name and fame of Penn,_____ Hear the

cheers go round the world_____ Cheer a - gain, boys, Her col-ors un-

furled_____ As we fight, with might, For fame and right, For - ev - ver true to

Penn - syl - va - ni - a._____ Fight for a. (Hoorah! Hoorah! Boom!)

Penn Glee Club's performance of spring show, *Casino* – 1979
Used with permission – Penn Glee Club

FOR PENN AND THE RED AND BLUE

Edgar M. Dilley, 1897, was the undergraduate leader of the Glee Club and J. A. Williams, 1909, was the president of the Combined Musical Clubs. They wrote this paean to Penn's flag for the 1909 Mask & Wig show, *Merely a Monarch*. While this song enjoyed brief popularity at the time, Mr. Dilley's name probably would be unknown to us today were it not for his better-known lyric to Penn's alma mater, "Hail Pennsylvania."

FOR PENN AND THE RED AND BLUE

Words by
EDGAR M. DILLEY 1897

Music by
J.A. WILLIAMS 1909

1. Though we'll love the stars and stripes for aye,
2. There are those who dream of eyes of blue;

As it waves o'er - head the live - long day,
Eyes of blue are fine, we think, don't you?

And no mat - ter what the world may say,
There are those who dream of lips of red,

123

There's no coun-try like the "U. S. A."
Lips of red are love - ly things, 'tis said.

Still un - to an-other - er flag we're true,
Tho' we nev - er dream of lips or eyes,

Un - der it we win our bat - tles, too,
It would not oc - ca - sion much sur - prise

Dear old Penn-sy's flag, boys, Is our grand old rag, boys,
If some day we might, boys, Dream-ing in the night, boys,

We will wave the Red and Blue._____
Lips and eyes are Red and Blue._____

Chorus

Penn - syl - va - nia, To our flag we're true,

Penn - syl - va - nia,___ And the Red and Blue, We'll keep it

fly - ing, Nev - er stop try - ing, For that flag and

you;_____ Penn - syl - va - nia, To our flag we're

true, Penn - syl - va - nia, And the Red and Blue;

Through thick and thin, boys,___ Go in and win, boys, For

Penn and the Red and Blue. Blue._____

UNIVERSITY OF PENNSYLVANIA CAFÉ

Words by
MARY HIBBS GEISLER 1902

Music by
J. DYNELEY PRINCE

1. In the old hash-house at col - lege, look-ing sad - ly from the plate, There's a
2. Take me back to Penn-sy's hash-house, where the best is like the worst, Where there

cus - tard pie a - set - ting, know - ing that it's to be ate; For the
ain't no ta - ble man - ners, and a man can raise a thirst; For the

din - ner's on the ta - ble, and the din - ner - bells they say, "Come you
din - ner - bells are call - ing, and it's there that I would be, I don't

A Mask and Wig Serenade
Used with permission – Mask and Wig

UNIVERSITY OF PENNSYLVANIA CAFÉ

I am somewhat baffled by the attributions given in the earlier Penn songbooks in which this song is printed. In the little volume entitled *Pennsylvania's Verse* – which was verses only, sans music – published in 1902, Mary Hibbs Geisler first presents her poem "with apologies to Rudyard Kipling." Certainly she used his "On the Road to Mandalay" as her model. The 1903 songbook includes her lyric with music attributed to a J. Dyneley Prince. But the 1923 edition – which was edited by a committee – claims that the words are set to the air of "On the Road to Mandalay." It then proceeds to print the melody by Prince instead of "On the Road to Mandalay." Not only is the music printed there not to the tune of that famous song, but it is impossible to sing the lyric to the familiar tune. It simply doesn't fit. So much for editing books "by committee!"

FRANKLIN FIELD MARCH

Edwin Franco Goldman's march has been the most elusive work in this entire songbook project. I knew of the piece only from its mention in George E. Nitzsche's article in the Franklin Field Illustrated of October 19, 1940. Searching for a copy of the music led from one dead-end to another until I was very nearly ready to give up on it. It was the very last missing piece of the jigsaw puzzle that this book had become and was holding up the entire volume from completion. Neither Penn's library or archives, nor the Philadelphia or New York public libraries, had any knowledge of the march. Andrew Flatt, manager of the Goldman Memorial Band in New York, couldn't help. The Goldman Band Library at the University of Iowa was equally in the dark. Even Gail L. Freunsch of the Music Division of the Library of Congress, which handles copyrights, hit a cul-de-sac and could suggest nowhere else to turn. Finally, Claude White, Penn's Band director until 1994, remembered that the Penn Wind Ensemble had played it many years earlier from then existing band parts; he was fairly certain that the concert had been recorded. The Music Department of Penn's Van Pelt Library was unable to come up with parts, but did find a rather poor audio cassette of that live performance. My next job, therefore, was to sit down with a copy of the tape and write out a full transcription for piano by ear. No sooner had I finished that task in July, 1995, when I remembered that Nietzsche mentioned in his article that he had written a lyric for the trio of the march. The search began all over again! The hero of the day was Hamilton Y. Elliott, Jr., associate director of the University Archives (who had also reached an impasse); while looking for something else entirely, Ham came across a manuscript for the "Franklin Field March" in a copyist's hand – containing a notation, signed by Goldman, that this was, indeed, the official manuscript! In addition, yet another hand had penciled in George Nitzsche's lyric. Ham had the savvy to recognize it, shift gears and immediately contact me. I had spent years looking for the march and, after finally spending numerous hours transcribing it from a poor tape, one month later the manuscript was discovered! The good news was that, in comparing Mr. Goldman's version and mine, virtually the only difference was that mine was in two-four time and his was in cut time! I was relieved to realize that I still had a pretty fair ear! The version published here, needless to say, is Goldman's – with only a few stylistic or harmonic changes. At its premiere on Franklin Field on November 5, 1932, the composer conducted the combined bands of Penn and the University of Pittsburgh. At that time, he dedicated his new work to the University of Pennsylvania. We must assume that the lyric was added later as it was not even mentioned in the hoopla in advance of the premiere, nor is any reference made to its performance by the combined bands in the day's program. Now that the "lost" march has at last been re-discovered, I hope its future will prove to be more propitious than its past. We should also hope it will only be played – not sung. Nietzsche's words did not do him justice!

FRANKLIN FIELD MARCH

Words by
GEORGE E. NITZSCHE 1898

Music by
EDWIN FRANKO GOLDMAN

Trio

To Penn - syl - van - - i - a our -

-selves we give._____ For thy_____ glo - ry_____

— and hon - or we shall live._____ Thy sons_____

132

to thee_____ for - ev - er shall be true._____

So fight!_____ Fight! Fight!_____ for dear old

Red and Blue._____

To Penn - - - syl - van - - i - a we'll

loy - al be._____ Thy great - - ness shall_____

_ re - sound from sea to sea._____ On Frank_____

_ lin Field_____ let's cheer our team and men_____

poco a poco cresc.

to Fight! Fight! Fight!

to vic - to - ry for Penn.

sffz

Penn Band formation on Franklin Field – Circa early 1950's
Used with permission – Penn Band Archives

PENNSYLVANIA'S FOOTBALL SONG

Words by
THOMAS B. DONALDSON 1899

Music by
CHARLES GILPIN III 1899

PENNSYLVANIA'S FOOTBALL SONG

For more than two decades at the beginning of the 20th century, Charles Gilpin III, Class of 1899, wrote the music – and often the lyrics, as well – for a string of highly successful Mask & Wig shows. Every Penn composer or author attempts to write a work that will endure as a popular fight song, drinking song or ballad. In this case, Donaldson and Gilpin surely hoped to write "the definitive football song." While it was a decided hit in their 1901 show *Baa, Baa, Black Sheep*, it never achieved widespread or lasting popularity.

Penn Glee Club in concert – 1970's
Used with permission – Penn Glee Club

PENN, PENNSYLVANIA

Isaac Hampshur Jones wrote the words to this song when he was the undergraduate leader of the Penn Glee Club. He set them to a tune that Jason Noble Pierce had written for Amherst College in 1903 – and, what's more, he did it with Pierce's permission. How marvelously ecumenical! While Jones speaks proudly of "do or die" and "always victorious, year after year," it is interesting to note that he has taken the precaution of adding a lyric that may be used "in case we lose!"

PENN, PENNSYLVANIA

Words by
ISAAC HAMPSHUR JONES 1906

Music by
JASON NOBLE PIERCE

Men of Penn, get to-geth-er once a-gain, In a good old rous-ing song, Staunch and true to the roy-al Red and Blue, With voi-ces clear and strong. "Do or die!" That will be our bat-tle cry, As we give our "long Hoo- rah." Then let us shout the

Chorus

cho-rus out For old Penn-syl-va - ni - a.

Penn, Penn - syl-va - nia, We've naught
*Penn, Penn - syl-va - nia, It's all

— to fear,— Al - ways— vic - to - rious, Year af -
— the same,— Win - ning or los - sing We're al -

- ter year!— So, boys,— to - geth - er We'll cheer
- ways game!— So, boys,— to - geth - er We'll cheer

(shouted) Rah! Rah! Rah!

— for - ev - er Penn, Penn — syl - va - ni — a!—

*In case we lose

142

UNIVERSITY OF PENNSYLVANIA
BICENTENNIAL MARCH

Words by
EDWARD FOLEY 1935

Music by
ROBERT DOANE 1942

March Tempo

Trio

Penn-syl - va - nia, now we cheer thee For the glo - ries that en-dear

thee To thy loy - al sons for - ev - er_____ Since the days of dear old Ben. And then, what the

years_____ to come may bring thee, Songs of praise_____ we'll ev-er sing thee. So we

144

UNIVERSITY OF PENNSYLVANIA BICENTENNIAL MARCH ⤳

As the University of Pennsylvania was preparing to celebrate its bicentennial in 1940, a contest was held for an official Bicentennial Song. Among the entries was this march, composed by Robert Doane, 1942, while he was an undergraduate in the School of Education. After completing the music, he asked his long-time friend and neighbor, Edward Foley, another Education major from the Class of 1935, to write lyrics to the trio of the piece. Foley, who had been president of the Glee Club during his senior year, obliged with his "Pennsylvania Salute" and their collaboration won the contest. When Mr. Foley delivered this music to me, he proudly wore a red and blue ribbon from which hung the bronze medallion especially sculpted for the bicentennial by the renowned Penn sculptor R. Tait McKenzie.

Penn Glee Club'ers rehearsing "bells"
Used with permission – Penn Glee Club

PENN RALLY SONG

Norman W. Harker, Class of 1908, and John L. Boyd, Class of 1910, were undergraduates when they wrote this predictable but spirited song. Harker was undergraduate leader of the Glee Club at the time.

PENN RALLY SONG

Words by
NORMAN W. HARKER 1908

Music by
JOHN L. BOYD 1910

Rather fast, with spirit

ff

Vamp till ready

1. Come, join your voic-es now for Penn-syl-va-nia,
2. To Al-ma Ma-ter dear, we pledge for-ev-er,

Cheer as in days gone by;_____ Ral-ly, ye sons of Penn, our
Till death we're true to thee,_____ Spir-it of dear old Penn shall

flag's un-furled, raise loud our bat-tle cry_____ Cheer_____
on-ward march, pro-claim-ing vic-to-ry_____ See,_____

147

those col - ors roy - al, boys, come ral - ly round _____ old Red and Blue, _____
a - bove those i - vied walls the same old flag _____ still waves a - bove, _____

To _____ that flag we're loy - al, boys, we'll fight for her _____
Nev - er in de - feat it falls, we'll e'er de - fend _____

Chorus

the bat - tle through. _____ Penn - - syl - va - ni -
that flag we love. _____

- a, thy sons stand true to thee, _____ High _____ thy

col - ors wave and point to vic - to - ry_____ Come, give a loud cheer for

Penn - syl - va - nia, Rah - hoo rah, that spir - it ne'er shall die_____

Hail, Penn - syl - va - ni - a, To thee our

song mounts high._____ high.

rit.

fff

LOYAL SONS OF PENN

       World War I was known as "the singing war." Men marched off to battle – or home from France – or just relaxed in barracks, to the tunes of George M. Cohan or Irving Berlin. Penn songs of this period reflect the pride felt by its students and faculty. Such songs as "Ave, Pennsylvania" and "Loyal Sons of Penn" belong to this group. Printed here as originally written, "Loyal Sons of Penn" was composed for baritone soloist and male chorus by H. Alexander Matthews, one of the most respected musicians of his day and longtime director of the Penn Glee Club.

LOYAL SONS OF PENN

Words by
DARRELL HEVENOR SMITH 1911

Music by
H. ALEXANDER MATTHEWS

Moderato e pomposo

Baritone Solo

1. Down thro' the years like re - ver - ber - ant thun_ der Ech - o the names of our
2. Through the fierce storm of a na - tion em - bat_ tled, Thou, Penn - syl - va - nia, hast

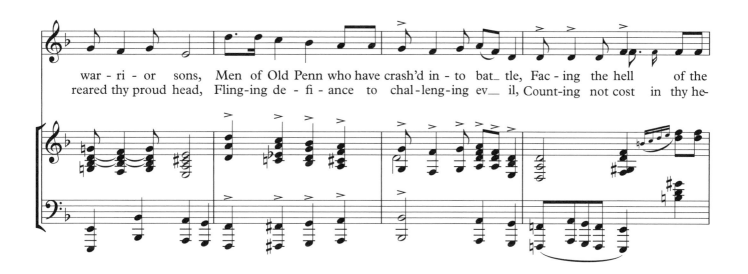

war - ri - or sons, Men of Old Penn who have crash'd in - to bat_ tle, Fac - ing the hell of the
reared thy proud head, Fling - ing de - fi - ance to chal - leng - ing ev_ il, Count - ing not cost in thy he-

shat-ter - ing guns.   Her - i - tage glo - ri - ous!   Phal-anx vic - tor - i - ous!
- ro - ic dead.   So   on through end - less days,   thy sons their voic - es raise,

On   with like   cour - age   ye sons of Old____ Penn,
Hail,____ Al - ma Ma - ter! Moth - er of Men!

Chorus

Her - i - tage____ glor - i - ous!   Phal-anx vic - tor - i - ous!   On   with like cour-age,   ye
So__on through end-less days,   thy sons their voic - es raise,

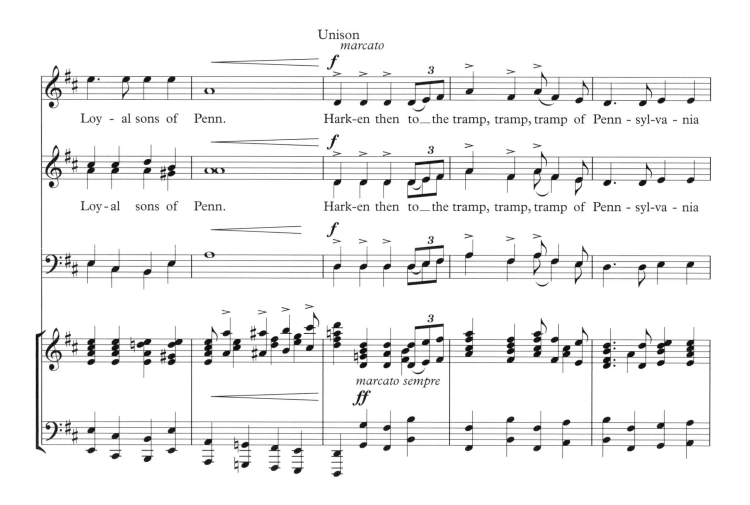

Loy - al sons of Penn. Hark-en then to the tramp, tramp, tramp of Penn - syl-va - nia men,

men, March-ing on in ser-ried ranks of bat-tle, Loy - al sons of Penn.

Heads up! Eyes front! Hats off to the Red and__

Heads up! Eyes front! Hats off to the Red and__

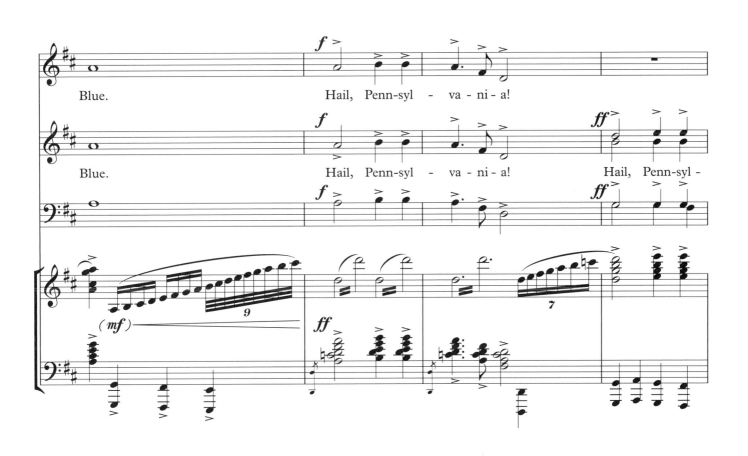

Blue. Hail, Penn-syl - va - ni - a!

Blue. Hail, Penn-syl - va - ni - a! Hail, Penn-syl -

As we tramp, tramp, tramp, The Loy - al sons of Penn, As we

-va - ni - a! As we tramp, tramp, tramp, The Loy - al sons of Penn, As we

tramp, tramp, tramp, tramp, tramp, tramp, tramp, The Loy - - al Sons of

tramp, tramp, tramp, tramp, tramp, tramp, tramp, The Loy - - al Sons of

rit.

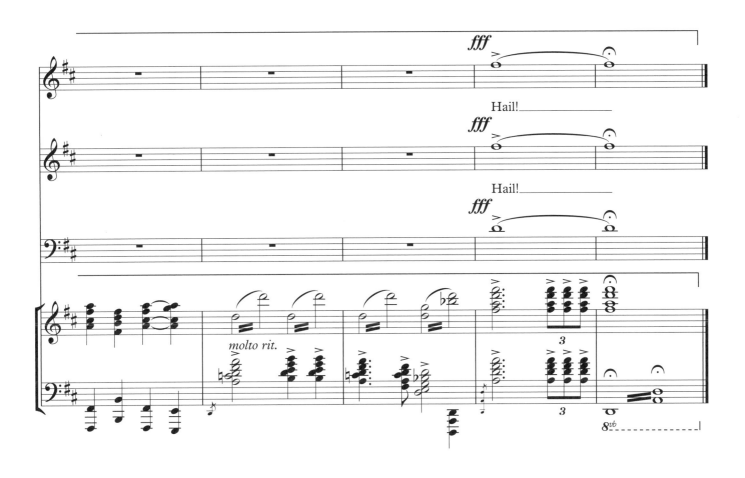

THE PENNSYLVANIA OAK

Words and music by
ARTHUR L. CHURCH 1878

1. In hope our wise fore-fa-thers set An a-corn in the earth,
2. Its stur-dy limbs have shel-tered well For many a fate-ful year,
3. Her cam-pus broad, her ter-rac-es Lie state-ly 'neath the sun;
4. These beau-ties mark the life with-in, As with their fra-grance rare,
5. Then let the Penn-syl-va-nian live High mind-ed and sin-cere,

From which a hard-y sap-ling sprang In vig-or from its birth.
Pro-fess-or, stu-dent, fel-low, all In cor-dial friend-ship here.
The gar-dens and half hid-den walk, How fair to look up-on!
The love-ly vi-o-let and rose Make sweet the balm-y air.
His pred-e-ces-sors call on him Their stan-dards to up-bear.

No drought de-stroyed the spread-ing roots, Nor gale its branch-es broke;
Full three and thir-ty thou-sand strong, A loy-al, stead-fast band;
Be-hold her cool and shad-ed lawns, Great gates and sculp-tured walls,
To teach the mind, the heart, the soul, Their pow-ers to ex-tend,
In no-ble em-u-la-tion with His fel-low col-lege men,

158

The tree of knowl-edge proved in time A strong and might - y oak.
They've made old Penn - syl - va - nia's name Re - sound from land to land.
And ris - ing proud - ly from the trees The loft - y, vice - clad halls.
Such wor - thy aims are Penn's i - deal, And shall be with - out end.
Let him aim well and strive to be The use - ful cit - i - zen.

Chorus

Three cheers for Penn - syl - va - ni - a, Give three and three times three;

No storm nor drought nor i - cy blast Shall harm that old oak tree.

THE PENNSYLVANIA OAK

Dedicated to Provost Charles C. Harrison, this sturdy metaphoric ode was written and composed in 1906 by Arthur L. Church, Class of 1878, according to its copyright. It made its first appearance in the 1909 edition of the Penn songbook.

Penn Glee Club in concert – 1950's
Used with permission – Penn Glee Club

PENN GLEE CLUB GRACE

Whenever the University of Pennsylvania Glee Club has a meal together, at home or on the road, it sings this grace before being seated. When I was seeking a non-sectarian text to set to music for this purpose, it was the Reverend Stanley E. Johnson, former chaplain of the University, who suggested these beautiful words from the fifteenth and sixteenth verses of Psalm 145. It was first performed by the Glee Club at their Award of Merit Banquet honoring the eminent conductor, Robert Shaw, on February 26, 1965. As with several other songs in this book, I have included a vocal solo-piano reduction along with the original version for *a cappella* male voices. An arrangement for *a cappella* mixed voices is also included.

PENN GLEE CLUB GRACE

Words from Psalm 145, Verses 15 and 16
For Male Chorus

Music by
BRUCE MONTGOMERY

PENN GLEE CLUB GRACE

Words from Psalm 145, Verses 15 and 16
For Mixed Chorus

Music by
BRUCE MONTGOMERY

PENN GLEE CLUB GRACE

Words from Psalm 145, Verses 15 and 16

Music by
BRUCE MONTGOMERY

Chorus line of Mask and Wig 58th Annual Production, *John Paul Jones* – 1946
Used with permission – Mask and Wig

MEN OF PENNSYLVANIA

Female students and alumnae of the University can find justifiable fault with a number of the songs of Penn mentioning men to their own exclusion. I can only hope that they will realize that the vast majority of Penn songs were written long ago in less enlightened times when the University was a predominantly male-oriented institution. As with so many of this country's most treasured documents and anthems, however, the references in most of the songs in this book – even Clay Boland's "Men of Pennsylvania" – should be considered generic and may be sung with equal pride by all. There are some Penn songs that never enjoyed great popularity but that still hang on. I don't believe anyone would ever know that Clay Boland wrote this song were it not included in the seven-song medley of Penn songs that the Glee Club sings – and in the two-song signature following each Mask & Wig performance. Understandably, the women on campus don't sing it very often.

MEN OF PENNSYLVANIA

Words and Music by
CLAY BOLAND 1926

165

SONG AND JIG

Author unknown

Composer unknown
Arranged by BRUCE MONTGOMERY

We've done our song and jig__ For dear old Mask and Wig,__ It's time to

say "good-bye"__ a - gain. We hope you're sat-is - fied__

And laughed un - til you cried,__ It's time to say "good- bye"__ a - gain.__

We hur-ry back each fall__ To heed re-hear-sal's call,__ We glad-ly give our all__ and we

love it. When all is said and done,— There's on-ly room for one.—

So lift your glass-es high,— Here's mud right in your eye!—

It's time to say "good-bye" a-gain.————

SONG AND JIG

Try as I may, I have been unable to determine who wrote this signature song for Mask & Wig – or when! For many years it has been sung as a curtain call following each performance by the troupe and it segues directly into "Men of Pennsylvania." It immed-iately precedes that humorous moment when the "women" remove their long wigs so that we may recognize the men playing the female roles. There was a marvelous reversal of this during the 1970's when some of the men playing the roles of men took off their short-cropped wigs to reveal their own natural long hair.

INTEGER VITAE

Words by
QUINTUS HORATIUS FLACCUS

Music by
FRIEDRICH F. FLEMMING

Andante

Lyrics (verse 1 / verse 2):

In - te - ger vi - tae sce - le - ris - que pu - rus non e - get Mau - ris
Si - ve per Syr - tis i - ter aes - tu - o - sas si - ve fac - tu - rus

ia - cu - lis, nec ar - cu nec ve - ne - na - tis
per in - hos - pi - ta - lem Cau - ca - sum vel___ quae

gra - vi - da sa - git - tis, Fus - ce, pha - re - tra.
lo - ca fa - bu - lo - sus lam - bit Hy - das - pes.

INTEGER VITAE

This is an 18th century student song and is known – like "Gaudeamus Igitur" – to student choruses throughout the world. The text is from the twenty-second Ode of Horace (Quintus Horatius Flaccus) and the music was composed by Friedrich F. Flemming (1778-1813). "Integer Vitae" was sung in the very first public concert ever given by the University of Pennsylvania Glee Club on May 23, 1864.

THE RED AND BLUE

This, of course, is the song that is unique among all college songs with its rhythmic waving of arms and hats during the chorus. This uniqueness has been somewhat diluted by the fact that, with the possible exceptions of "Fight On, Pennsylvania!" and Cornell's "Far Above Cayuga's Waters" (which, in fact, was an earlier song called "Annie Lisle" written in 1857 by H. S. Thompson), this famous Penn song has been more frequently copied and adapted to other colleges, schools, summer camps, etc., than almost any other collegiate song. It is a remarkable sight to see thousands of Penn fans at a football game – or any other sport, for that matter – waving their arms in perfect synchronization. William J. Goeckel composed the music in 1896 while he was the student leader of the Glee Club during his last year of Law School. Harry E. Westervelt added the verses a year later. During the 1980's "The Red and Blue" gradually began to replace "Hail, Pennsylvania" (Penn's acknowledged alma mater) at most official University functions. However, today it has become the Penn song most often used on such occasions. "Hail, Pennsylvania" is scarcely known anymore. In the 1990's, the first line "Come all ye loyal classmen now" was replaced with a more inclusive and acceptable "Come all ye loyal classmates now." While I generally don't condone changing an accepted song for reasons of "political correctness," this one seems logical and in no way changes the intent or the music of the song. Incidentally, please note that the correct title of this song is "The Red and Blue" – not "The Red and the Blue" as it so frequently and erroneously is identified.

THE RED AND BLUE

(original version, published in *Songs of the University of Pennsylvania*, 1903)

Words by
HARRY E. WESTERVELT 1898

Music by
WILLIAM J. GOECKEL 1896

★ The original lyric was "Come, all ye loyal classmen now"

171

Har - vard has her crim - son, Old Yale her col - ors too, But
ask no oth - er em - blem, No oth - er sign to view, We
knew that vic - t'ry then was ours, All else we might es - chew, If
wears them with a smile so bright, It wakes our hearts a - new, To
when to all our col - lege life We've said our last a - dieu, We'll

rit.

for dear Penn - syl - va - ni - a, We wear the Red and Blue.
on - ly ask to see and cheer Our co - lors Red and Blue.
on - ly we could wave and sing Our co - lors Red and Blue.
swear e - ter - nal loy - al - ty, To dear old Red and Blue.
ne - ver say a - dieu to thee, Our co - lors Red and Blue.

Chorus
ff

Hur - rah, Hur - rah, Penn - syl - va - ni - a, Hur - rah for the Red_ and the Blue; Hur-

rit. *a tempo* D.S.

-rah, Hur - rah, Hur - rah, Hur - rah, Hur - rah for the Red and Blue.

172

THE RED AND BLUE

(Mixed chorus)

Words by
HARRY E. WESTERVELT 1898

Music by
WILLIAM J. GOECKEL 1896
arr. BRUCE MONTGOMERY

Come, all ye loy - al class-mates now, In hall and cam-pus through, Lift up your hearts and

voi - ces for The roy - al Red and Blue. Fair Har-vard has her crim - son, Old

Yale her col - ors too, But for dear Penn-syl - va - ni - a, We wear the Red and

Blue. Hur - rah, Hur - rah, Penn-syl - va - ni - a, Hur - rah for the Red and the

Blue; Hur - rah, Hur - rah, Hur - rah, Hur - rah, Hur - rah for the Red and Blue.

THE RED AND BLUE

(Male chorus)

Words by
HARRY E. WESTERVELT 1898

Music by
WILLIAM J. GOECKEL 1896
arr. BRUCE MONTGOMERY

Come, all ye loy - al class-mates now, In hall and cam-pus through, Lift up your hearts and

voi - ces for The roy - al Red and Blue. Fair Har-vard has her crim - son, Old

Yale her col - ors too, But for dear Penn-syl - va - ni - a, We wear the Red and

Blue._____ Hur - rah, Hur-rah, Penn-syl - va - ni - a, Hur-rah for the Red_ and the

Blue;_____ Hur - rah, Hur - rah, Hur - rah, Hur - rah, Hur-rah for the Red and Blue.

THE RED AND BLUE

Words by
HARRY E. WESTERVELT 1898

Music by
WILLIAM J. GOECKEL 1896

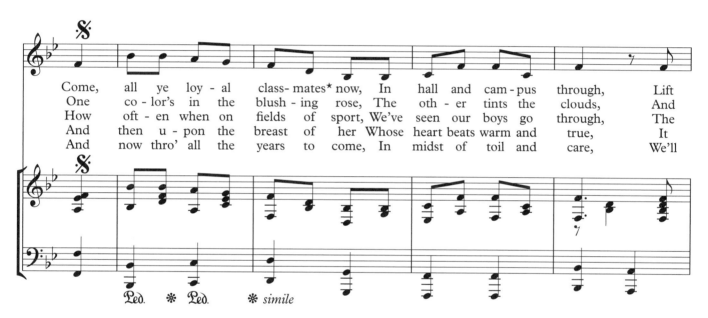

Come, all ye loy - al class-mates* now, In hall and cam-pus through, Lift
One co - lor's in the blush - ing rose, The oth - er tints the clouds, And
How oft - en when on fields of sport, We've seen our boys go through, The
And then u - pon the breast of her Whose heart beats warm and true, It
And now thro' all the years to come, In midst of toil and care, We'll

up your hearts and voi - ces for The roy - al Red and Blue. Fair
when to - geth - er both dis - close, We're hap - py as the gods. We
ve - ry air was rent in twain With cheers for Red and Blue. We
is the dear - est sight of all To see our Red and Blue. She
get new in - spi - ra - tion from The co - lors wa - ving there. And

The original lyric was "Come, all ye loyal classmen now"

175

Har - vard has her crim - son, Old Yale her col - ors too, But
ask no oth - er em - blem, No oth - er sign to view, We
knew that vic - t'ry then was ours, All else we might es - chew, If
wears them with a smile so bright, It wakes our hearts a - new, To
when to all our col - lege life We've said our last a - dieu, We'll

for dear Penn - syl - va - ni - a, We wear the Red and Blue.
on - ly ask to see and cheer Our col - ors Red and Blue.
on - ly we could wave and sing Our col - ors Red and Blue.
swear e - ter - nal loy - al - ty, To dear old Red and Blue.
ne - ver say a - dieu to thee, Our col - ors Red and Blue.

ff Chorus

Hur - rah, Hur - rah, Penn - syl - va - ni - a, Hur - rah for the Red and the Blue;

ff

D.S.

Hur - rah, Hur - rah, Hur - rah, Hur - rah, Hur - rah for the Red and the Blue.

D.S.

AFTERGLOW

Words and Music by
BRUCE MONTGOMERY

Slow and nostalgic

Sha-dows grow long on the cam-pus, twi-light has come a - again. Warm cop-per rays streak the

gold - en haze as peace set-tles down on Penn. And soft and low, in the pale af-ter-glow, the

voi-ces of stu-dents ring with the songs and cheers of their fair col-lege years, the songs they love to sing:

AFTERGLOW

This song was designed to bring a frankly sentimental tear of nostalgia to the cheek of even the most callous alumnus! It was written purposely to sound like a typical 19th century student song – although I hope it is more interesting harmonically than most of that genre. It was performed first by the Penn Glee Club at a Benjamin Franklin Associates dinner in January, 1965. I never could have predicted at that time that it would become the virtual "theme song" of the Glee Club – and perhaps more especially, the Glee Club Graduate Club ("GCGC"). Every social gathering of the Glee Club and the GCGC ends with the singing of "Afterglow," and many tears have been shed during renditions by alumni returning to campus or seniors about to leave. Although a vocal-piano version was prepared for this songbook so that it can be sung by anyone around the piano, the intended original sound is best accomplished by *a cappella* male voices.

AFTERGLOW
(Male Chorus)

This is the original version as composed
for the Penn Glee Club

Words and music by
BRUCE MONTGOMERY

Songs included in earlier Penn Songbook editions
but not included in Songs of Penn

Ah, Pennsylvania: 1903

Aladdin: 1923 (Mask & Wig)

Ancient Mariner, An: 1879

Annie Laurie: 1903

Antrim County Ball, The: 1903, 1909, 1916

Bring the Wagon Home, John: 1916

Bull-Dog, The: 1879, 1903

Capital Ship, A: 1903

Carmen: 1879

Carry Me Back to Pennsylvania: 1923

Class Song, '69: 1879

Class Song, '71: 1879

Class Song, '72: 1879

Class Song, '77: 1879

Class Song, '78: 1879

Class Song, '79: 1879

College Boys: 1879

College Hymn: 1879

College Life: 1879

College Song: 1879

College Stein Song: 1909, 1916

Commencement Hymn, A: 1903

Cremation Song of '81: 1879

Crew Song, The: 1903, 1909, 1923

Days of the Past, The: 1909, 1916

Demonstration, A: 1903

Down by the Stream: 1916

Drink to Me Only With Thine Eyes: 1903

Drinking Song: 1903

Ebeneezer: 1923 (Mask & Wig)

Examination Pie: 1879

Farewell Song, Class of '70: 1879

Farewell Song, '71: 1879

Fill Up Your Glasses: 1903, 1909, 1916, 1923 (Mask & Wig)

Forsaken: 1903

Forward, Pennsylvania: 1909, 1916

Fountain of Youth, The: 1923 (Mask & Wig)

Gallant Young Attorney, The: 1879

Gallant Young Freshman, The: 1879

Good Old Days at Penn, The: 1923

Good-Night, Ladies!: 1903

Hark, I Hear a Voice: 1903

He Was Nervous: 1903

Health to Old Penn: 1903, 1909, 1916, 1923

Here's to Old Penn: 1879, 1903,1909, 1916, 1923

Honey, Dat I Love So Well: 1916

I Arise From Dreams of Thee: 1903

In the Shade of Her Pink Parasol: 1909, 1916

Jingle, Bells: 1903

Jolly Boating Weather: 1903

Jolly Miller, The: 1903

Juanita: 1903

Last Cigar (My): 1879, 1903

Last Night: 1903

Lauriger Horatius: 1879, 1903, 1909, 1916,

Levee Song: 1903, 1916

Life Lesson, A: 1916

Line Up, There! Pennsylvania!: 1923

Little Quaker Maid: 1923 *(Mask & Wig)*

Little Red Riding Hood: 1923 *(Mask & Wig)*

Lone Fish-Ball, The: 1903, 1916

Loreley, The: 1903

Love Will Find a Way of its Own: 1923 *(Mask & Wig)*

Lullaby Serenade: 1903, 1909, 1916, 1923 *(Mask & Wig)*

Mamie's Charms: 1903

Maria's Lambkin: 1879

Mary Had a William Goat: 1903, 1909, 1916, 1923

Mary Jane: 1903

Mermaid, The: 1879

My Bonnie: 1903

My Old Kentucky Home: 1903

Never-Study Club, The: 1923

Nut Brown Maiden: 1903

Old (Man) Noah: 1879, 1916

Old College Cheer: 1903

Old College Chum: 1903

Old Penn: 1879

Old Pennsylvania Memories: 1923

Old Pennsylvania, Mother Dear: 1923

On the Chapel Steps: 1916

Onward, Pennsylvania: 1909, 1916, 1923

Our Lovely Times: 1879

Peanuts: 1879

Pennsylvania Stein Song: 1903, 1909, 1916, 1923

Pennsylvania, Do: 1909, 1916

Peter Gray: 1903

Play Ball! 1903, 1909, 1916

Pope, The: 1903

Quilting Party, The: 1903

Quintus Horatius Flaccus: 1903, 1909

Respice, Circumspice: 1909, 1916

Reunion Song: 1909, 1916, 1923

Rosalie: 1903

Serenade ('79): 1879

Serenade ('81): 1879, 1903

She Answered Me Nay: 1903

Simon the Cellarer: 1903

Slattery's Mounted Foot: 1903

Smoker's Anthem: 1903

Soldier's Farewell: 1903

Somewhere in France: 1923

Song of the Pipe: 1923 (Mask & Wig)

Song of the Red and the Blue, A: 1909, 1916, 1923

Further information may be obtained about these songs through the
Archives of the University of Pennsylvania

Acknowledgements
by Bruce Montgomery [2008]

One of the irresistible by-products of working at the University of Pennsylvania for as long as I did (at this writing I am officially "retired" but back on campus regularly and still directing the Penn Singers in light opera every Spring) is that, through sheer longevity, one simply must have developed into an expert at *something*. If, after directing the Penn Glee Club for forty-four years in thirty countries on five continents, I have gained any unavoidable expertise, it would have to be through my familiarity with the many songs of the University.

I have arranged a multitude of them for chorus and I have no way of estimating the number of times I've conducted them but it conservatively numbers in the thousands. So I guess statistics alone would have pointed to me to be the one to edit and arrange this new edition of Penn songs.

Many different avenues had to be traveled to obtain some of the information contained in this volume and to verify names, dates, spellings and classes of the various authors and composers of the songs of Penn. I am greatly indebted to a number of individuals and offices for such assistance, most particularly to:

Michel T. Huber, *former Executive Secretary of the General Alumni Society who for years has kept me supplied with all sorts of valuable tidbits relating to Penn songs and their backgrounds. Much of the time his input has been purposeful, with this book in the back of his mind. Other times his suggestions have arisen in informal conversation. But being something of a squirrel at heart, I have stored away each nut of information to finally find its place here.*

David Zoob, *with whom I carried on a most pleasant correspondence and who seemed modestly surprised that one of his student endeavors has remained one of our Penn classics.*

Marshall Bartholomew, *for so many years the director of the Yale Glee Club and one of the most knowledgeable experts in collegiate songs who ever lived, who generously shared his expertise with me over many years of friendship.*

Claude White, *former Director of the Penn Band and the University Symphony, who in addition to being a fine musician, for years gave me his counsel and supplied several items for this volume.*

Shelly Z. Green, *General Counsel of the University, and* *Debra Fickler*, *Assistant General Counsel – both holding those positions at the time I began this book – who so willingly gave me their legal advice as it pertained to contracts and copyrights.*

Anthony A. Lyle, *former Editor of the* Pennsylvania Gazette, *who supported so many of my endeavors at Penn and who let his many readers follow the slow progress of this volume.*

Samuel Hughes, *current Editor of the* Pennsylvania Gazette, *who took right up where Tony left off.*

The late *Donald T. Sheehan*, *former Director of Public Relations, who in 1954 started my fascination with Penn songs and traditions in the first place.*

The five University of Pennsylvania presidents whom I have had the privilege and pleasure of knowing as friends: **Gaylord P. Harnwell**, **Martin Meyerson**, **Sheldon Hackney**, **Claire Fagin** *(Interim President)* and **Judith Rodin** *– each of whose support of music on campus and the tradition of singing Penn songs always has been deeply appreciated.*

Jeffrey Coon, *College 1992 and* **Robert Penn Biron**, *College 1991, former students in the Penn Glee Club who, as undergraduates, did considerable leg-work and typing for me in the earliest stages of this book.*

Stephen Goff, *former Managing Director of the Annenberg Center, who was a valued confidante on much that I did at Penn from 1964 on and who helped find several elusive items for this book.*

The Office of Alumni Records, *who unfailingly helped me check current addresses and graduation dates of alumni composers and authors.*

The Library of Congress, *the* **Free Library of Philadelphia**, *the* **New York Public Library** *and the* **Van Pelt Library** *at the University of Pennsylvania for their valuable cooperation and friendly assistance.*

Mark Frazier Lloyd *and* **Hamilton Y. Elliott, Jr.**, *of the University Archives, for painstaking searches for material included in this volume.*

Ronald Shapiro *and his fine* **Campus Copy Center** *for printing drafts of this book to be submitted to publishers.*

And finally, and most especially, to the **University of Pennsylvania** *itself – its students, its faculty, its administration, its staff of devoted workers, and its alumni. All have given me a life of such happiness that for fifty years I blessed them each morning for the opportunity to begin a new day at that great institution. If that characterizes me as Pollyanna, so be it!*

Additional Acknowledgements from the Bruce Montgomery Foundation for the Arts

A band of devoted volunteers has worked tirelessly to bring this project to fruition. By choosing to self-publish, the Foundation is able to allocate all revenues from sales of *Songs of Penn* to the Fellowships & Grants program of its endowment. It is with highest regard and deepest gratitude that we acknowledge the following individuals:

Michel Huber, *former Executive Director of Alumni Affairs, and* **Nicholas Constan**, *Adjunct Professor, Wharton, who were among the first catalysts for this project and who urged the Bruce Montgomery Foundation to publish Monty's eagerly-awaited songbook posthumously.*

Dr. Amy Gutmann, *President of the University of Pennsylvania, and Christopher H. Browne Distinguished Professor of Political Science, for contributing her generous foreword to* Songs of Penn.

Medha Narvekar, Associate Vice President for Development and Alumni Relations; *F. Hoopes Wampler*, Assistant Vice President Alumni Relations; *Elise Betz*, Executive Director Alumni Relations; *Lisbeth Willis*, Director, Classes & Reunions, Alumni Relations; *Ilene Wilder*, Director of Marketing and Business Development; *Ty A. Furman*, Ed.D, former Director, University Life (VPUL) Arts Initiatives; and *Troy Majnerick*, Associate Director, Office of New Student Orientation and Academic Initiatives – for their enthusiastic and vital support of this project from the beginning.

Todd Shotz (College 1996), former President of the Penn Glee Club, who chaired the Songbook Committee. His assistance in editing text and spearheading the Foundation's fundraising efforts for this project has been invaluable.

C. Erik Nordgren, Ph.D. GSAS 2001, Monty's handpicked successor as Director of the Penn Glee Club, for volunteering his leadership to the arduous task of music engraving and converting fifty-five songs into 21st century technology for printing. His superb editing skills, his familiarity with the repertoire, his musicianship, and his unwavering devotion of time and energy to this project have been priceless.

Kushol Gupta, Ph.D., Assistant Director, Penn Band, for reaching out to the Foundation to volunteer his valuable time and considerable musical and computer skills to engraving and editing. His generosity in sharing his extensive knowledge of Penn's music history and repertoire with the Foundation – and his assistance in gathering visual materials and permissions for use in this book – are greatly appreciated. Without Kushol and Erik this project would have been infinitely more difficult to accomplish.

Greer Cheeseman, Director of the Penn Band, for his professional assistance with music engraving, and for his help and expertise in spreading the word that Songs of Penn is finally being published.

Our student and recent-graduate team of music engravers, including *John Palusci* (College 2009); *Jon Urban* (College 2013); *Scott Ventre* (College 2013); and *Ned Cunningham* (College 2012). Their technical wizardry and willing assistance contributed greatly to our ability to meet crucial deadlines.

Florrie Marks, current Musical Director of the Penn Singers' annual Gilbert & Sullivan operettas, and revered colleague of Monty, for her musical talent, her assistance with engraving, and her indomitable spirit in all she does.

Robert Hallock (Wharton 1971), Glee Club Graduate Club, whose musicianship as a choral arranger and solo performer enhances his proofreading and editing skills. His dedication and support have been vital to the success of this project.

Marc Mostovoy, Founder and Conductor Emeritus of the Chamber Orchestra of Philadelphia, for his unfailing support as a board member of the Bruce Montgomery Foundation for the Arts, and for his assistance and wise counsel during editing. His contribution has been invaluable.

Jenny Young, Creative Director, ADVERTISING Without The Agency, for her generous gift of friendship and expertise in layout and design. It is she who has made it possible for the Foundation to self-publish its first project with professional flair and pride.

Nicholas B. Thomas, Jr., Monty's nephew, for his design of the Foundation's logo and the dust jacket of Songs of Penn.

Susan Poliniak (College 1991), former Penn Singer, whose background in music publishing and editing afforded us a "crash course" in music engraving so that we could self-publish with confidence.

Mark Frazier Lloyd, Director, University Archives and Records Center; *Alumni Relations; Campus Communications; Stephen Goff,* Former Managing Director, Annenberg Center for the Performing Arts and Archivist for Mask & Wig; and *Charles McClelland* (2014), Vice President, Penn Glee Club, for their collective generosity in seeking, obtaining and granting permission to reproduce certain songs and images in Songs of Penn. Mark Lloyd's confirmation that most of the material contained herein is now in the public domain (with the exception of original music by Bruce Montgomery) was "music to our ears!" Monty's original songs are copyrighted and owned by the Bruce Montgomery Foundation for the Arts and are used in Songs of Penn *with permission.*

Samuel Hughes, Senior Editor of The Pennsylvania Gazette, *whose support of Monty's endeavors – during his life and after his passing – have made a significant difference.*

Gene Schneyer (College 1975), Penn Glee Club Graduate Club; and *William B. Kelley*, Jr., Honorary Glee Cub Member; *Melinda Thomas, Vicki Thomas Pohl,* and *Susan Montgomery Thomas Burke, for reviewing final proofs before going to press along with* *Nicholas B. Thomas, Monty's brother-in-law, for his unfailing support, encouragement, patience and sense of humor throughout this project.*

Special thanks go to the Foundation's **Board of Directors** *for their enthusiastic support of our decision to establish a new 501(c)(3) not-for-profit public charity during uncertain economic times. On behalf of Bruce Montgomery's family, I want to thank the Board for their devotion to Monty and for their kindness to me personally during the first two years of the Foundation's existence.*

Finally – and most gratefully – to all of the generous **Sponsors** *of this book (see "Noteworthy Supporters"– page 187). They have demonstrated their love for music, for Monty, and for the University of Pennsylvania in an extraordinary way.* Songs of Penn *has sprung to life because of their financial support.*

Editor
Elizabeth Montgomery Thomas
Executive Director, BMFA

Noteworthy Supporters

The Bruce Montgomery Foundation for the Arts gratefully acknowledges the following benefactors whose generous sponsorship has made possible the completion of *Songs of Penn*.
These individuals clearly honored Monty's timeless adage:
"Don't be afraid to be magnificent!"

Alma Mater

Julie & Marc Platt

College Hall

Joseph J. Hill

Locust Walk

Anne Middleton Flood

Molly & Mitch Mudick, *PGC President 1973-75*

Wendell R. Ware

Franklin Field

Richard & Nora Berlinger

Robert Penn Biron, Esq. & Dr. Karen B. Zur

Parker & Joan Quillen
In Memory of Frank F. Brierly

Colonel Timothy E. & Amy L. Dunster

Barry E. Bressler & Betty Gross Eisenberg

The Lily Foundation

Helen McLaughlin
In Memory of Peter Aloysius McLaughlin

Lyn & David Montgomery

Chris, Christopher & Vicki Thomas Pohl

Jennifer, Jack & Ella Ross

Nicholas & Elizabeth Montgomery Thomas

Jena, Emily & Nicholas B. Thomas, Jr.

Todd Shotz, *PGC President 1995-96*, & Family

Gregory S. Suss & Family

William C. Tost, Jr.

Red & Blue

Harvey J. Bellin, M.D.

Peter A. Benoliel & Willo Carey

Janet & Larry Carroll

Charles & Carol Cox

Scott Davenport

In Memory of James DePreist

Charles L. Fishman, *C'83*

David J. Goldsmith, *PGC President 1992-93*

Pouya Hatam, D.M.D., *D'95*

Andrew S. Janet

Ann Kaminski & Michael Albus

Ruth Sarah Lee, *In Memory of Dr. Charles Lee*

The Lindner Family

Drs. Michael Manolas & Jennie Barbieri

Keith L. Neal, *W '68*

Edwin & Katherine Nealley

Nancy & David (Buzz) Neusteter

Aki J. Peritz

Jefrey I. Pollock

Governor Edward G. Rendell

Marilyn & Michael Rutner *Philanthropic Fund of the Dallas Jewish Community Foundation*

John J. Scarborough, Jr., *PGC President 1972-73*

Debra Appel, *CW'75* & Gene Schneyer *C'75*

Eve & Fred Simon Charitable Foundation

Gail & Edward Snitzer

Edward (Skip) Swikart III, *PGC President 1979-80*

Melinda S. Thomas

Linda V. Troost, Ph. D.

David Vaughn

Bradford Wilson

David M. Zlotchew

Toast To Penn

Lydia Nassima Abdo

Albert M. Adams, *Ed.D.*

Michael Adelstein

Wayne Baruch, *PGC President*

Charles, *C'73* & Gail *GEd '84*, Battista

Ambassador (Ret.) Robert M. Beecroft, *C'62, G'65*

Jerald M. Berkowitz, *FAS '79*

Dr. George E. & Mrs. Carol H. Biron

Stanford and Susan Montgomery Thomas Burke

Robert A. Busser, *C'60*

Chas & Amanda Carol

Dolores Ferraro Cascarino

Alexandra Chalif & David Thomson

Daniel H. Coelho, M.D

Constance Montgomery Cook

Phyllis & John Richard Cook, Jr.

Jeffrey Coon, *PGC President 1991-02*

Lee Ross Crain, *PGC President 2009-10,* & Family, *In Memory of Dr. Richard M. Crain*

Robert Croll, *PGC President 2011-12*

Susannah Engstrom & Christopher C. Cyr, *PGC President 2001-02*

Ned Cunningham, *C'12*

Gigi & Allan Dash

Daniel S. Dent

Stephen J. DiGregoria, *PGC President 2013-14*

S. David Eisenberg

Joshua D. Eisenberg

Tish Emerson

Richard Engel, M.D.

Alexander P. Feldman, *PGC President 2003-05*

Randall & Madelaine Feldman

Jonathan T. Ferrari & Family

William Kohn Fleissig

Jon Gailmor, *PGC President 1969-70*

Chris Geczy

Mark Glassman

Thomas & Marguerite Godbold

Marguerite & Steve Goff

Joan & David Green

Jon & Mary Ann Greenawalt

Sherry & Brian Greenberg

James R. Guthrie, *PGC President 1961-62*

Jeff Hahn

Elizabeth & Tom Haller

Fritzi K. & Robert J. Hallock, *PGC President 1970-71*

Beth & Ronald L. Hjelm, *C'78*

Steve "The Whistler" Herbst, *C'67*

Ron Hirasawa

David L. Hopkins, *W'83*

Barbara & Michel Huber

Mark Huerta, *PGC President 2008-09*

Hugh A. Jones, Esq.

Mark Jordan

Jacque & Eddie Kamarauskas

Daniel M. Katz, Esq.

William B. Kelley, Jr., *'78*

Byron Kho

Darren Klein, *Inspire Human Resources*

Elie Landau, *C'94*

Margo & Franz Lassner

Miles Cary Leahey & Patricia C. Mosser

Michele Leff

Victoria & Christopher LeVine

Tucker Levy

Peggy & Rob Roy MacGregor

Brian Maloney

Richard K. & Julie C. May

James D. Mendelsohn

Charles M. Meredith III

Martha H. Morris

Marc Mostovoy & Mi-Young Park

Barton & Victoria Myers

Judith F. Nelson

Christopher G. Neuhaus

April & Brendan O'Brien, *PGC President 1986-87*

Conor & Dawn P. O'Croinin

Elizabeth Stafford Luttrell Offutt

Jonathan Ozark, *PGC President 2002-03*

Roslyn & Vincent Palusci, *C'80*

Brian R. Percival

Daniel Pincus, *'00*

Eduardo Placer, *PGC President 1998-99*

Allan T. Polischak

The Quereau/Roberts Family

Elsa & Bill Ramsden

John Reardon, *President Penn Alumni Society, 1992-95*

Bradley Richards

Scott Romeika, *PGC President 1993-94*

Edward J. & Evelyn Rosen, *Philanthropic Fund of the Jewish Federation of Greater Philadelphia*

Donn Rubin

Simone Sallé

The Schinfeld Family *in memory of Sandy*

William M. Schmidt, *W '69*

Barry Scott

Afterword

Bruce "Monty" Montgomery was my dear friend and mentor for sixteen years,
from nearly the day I first arrived at Penn in 1992, until his passing in 2008.
When he decided to retire – after 50 years of service to the University – it was
my happy fortune to be in the right place at the right time.
In fact, one of my life's proudest moments occurred at his retirement gala
in April 2000 when Monty publicly announced that he and the Penn administration
had selected me to be his successor as Director of the Penn Glee Club.

Having served in that role now for thirteen years and counting, I consider it my
professional duty to preserve and promote a greater knowledge
of Penn's musical treasures and traditions amongst the extended family
of the University: her students, alumni, parents, staff and faculty.
In that light, it has been my distinct honor and privilege to help bring
this important manuscript to fruition, for the entertainment
and edification of Pennsylvanians everywhere.

It is my fervent hope – with a nod to our Founder, Benjamin Franklin –
that this volume of music, history and photographs will serve as
a "most useful and most ornamental" addition to the home of every
"Pennsylvania Girl" and all the "Men of Pennsylvania", be they young or old, near or far.
And to borrow from Monty's own "Afterglow:" may we all forevermore
"Sing the praise of college days; Sing of Pennsylvania!"

C. Erik Nordgren
Director, University of Pennsylvania Glee Club
2000 - present

"Don't be afraid to be magnificent!"

Bruce Montgomery

Premiere performance of "The Penn Glee Club March (Penny Whistle)"
by Bruce Montgomery
Homecoming · 25 October 1986 · Franklin Field · Philadelphia · Pa.
Performed by the Penn Band & Penn Glee Club · The composer directing.

Penn Glee Club in concert - Monty conducting
Used with permission of Penn Glee Club

Mask and Wig singing "Red and Blue" - 123rd annual production: *A Volcanic Eruption*
Used with permission of Mask and Wig

Penn Band at Franklin Field - Pulaski Day
Used with permission of Penn Band

Monty conducting Penn Glee Club at an informal occasion - 1990's
Used with permission of Penn Glee Club

"The Red and Blue" - Hey Day 2011
Used with permission of University Communications

"A Toast to Penn" toast throwing at Franklin Field
Used with permission of University Archives & Record Center - University of Pennsylvania

Spirit at the Penn Palestra
Used with permission of Athletic Communications

Penn Glee Club with "The Quaker" and Director C. Erik Nordgren - 2012
Used with permission of Penn Glee Club

March through campus - Hey Day 2011
Used with permission of University Communications

Drummers on Parade - Hey Day 2011
Used with permission of University Communications

21st Century model of "The Pennsylvania Girl" - Penn Band
Used with permission of Mickey Goldin, C'60, D'64

"Cheer, Pennsylvania!" - Franklin Field
Used with permission of Kushol Gupta, Assistant Director, Penn Band

Commencement Parade on campus
Used with permission of University Communications

Penn Glee Club sings "The Red and Blue" at Commencement
Used with permission of University Communications